Country
Weekend
Socks

COUNTRY WEEKEND SOCKS.

Printed in China.

For information, address St. Martin's Press,
175 Fifth Avenue, New York, N.Y. 10010.

www.stmartins.com

Library of Congress Cataloging-in-
Publication Data Available Upon Request

ISBN: 978-0-312-64422-2

First U.S. Edition: November 2010

10 9 8 7 6 5 4 3 2 1

Publisher Jacqui Small
Managing Editor Kerenza Swift
Project Editor Zia Mattocks
Art Director Barbara Zuñiga
Production Peter Colley

Photographer's Assistant Lauren Hutton
Stylist Stella Nicholaisen
Hair and Make-up Nuala McArdle

BMA Agency models Dan Corsi,
Sam Cunningham, Delina Ghezu,
Caroline Royce

Country Weekend Socks

25 classic patterns to knit

Madeline Weston

Photography by
Simon Brown

St. Martin's Griffin
New York

17

18

19

20

21

22

23

24

25

Contents

Introduction

My interest in knitting, especially the traditional knitting of the British Isles, began in the 1970s after my partner David Tomlinson and I had opened our shop, The Scottish Merchant, in Covent Garden, London. We stocked crafts from Scotland, including pottery, glass, and silver, as well as textiles. Shortly after we had opened, we made contact with Margaret Stuart in Shetland, who was organizing a group of knitters to knit the older, stronger Fair Isle patterns in the original colors, as well as shawls and lacy scarves in new color schemes.

We were also finding some of the last remaining fishermen's gansey knitters from the north-east coast of England, as well as the Outer Hebrides. These intricately patterned jerseys were masterpieces of the craft of the knitter, with their seamless construction, worked in the worsted 5-ply wool yarn.

It was soon obvious that our customers were delighted by the knitwear we had found, especially that from the Shetland Islands.

Unfortunately, over the years, the knitters from these small cottage industries and cooperatives have become fewer in number, the time involved in the work sometimes making the cost too high for the retail market. The good news is that home knitting has taken on a new lease on life, with a huge interest in the craft compensating for the falling-off of local production. What was once a skill that thrived because of necessity is now a form of creativity and relaxation for an enormous number of people.

As well as the home knitters' interest in the bright "designer" patterns that are the subject of many books and magazines, knitters have also found an interest in discovering the older patterns—even copying those in museums—and updating them for modern needs and tastes. Socks are some of the oldest pieces of knitting to have been discovered, and they are also extraordinarily popular and satisfying to knit.

As I hope this book shows, the variety of yarns, types of stitch patterns, colors, and methods of knitting are almost endless. Socks of some kind are worn by nearly everybody, and the pleasure of knitting socks by hand—and of wearing hand-knitted socks—cannot be denied.

Included here are some of the traditional patterns from around Britain and other parts of the world. Some have been given a new twist, but others are reproduced in their original, authentic form, so that you can make socks for yourself or your friends that are "the real thing." I have chosen yarns that are readily available—some soft and luxurious, some dense and hardwearing—and produced a collection of 25 patterns for hand-knitted socks, which show knitting styles familiar to us all. Cables, Fair Isle, Argyle, lace stitches, gansey stitches, and multicolored patterns adorn socks for wearing on country walks or while lounging on the sofa, which look as good with walking boots or wellingtons as they do with pretty dresses and heels. The possibilities are endless.

I have trawled through patterns from Scotland, Ireland, Turkey, and Egypt; I have searched vintage patterns for inspiration, and sought the expertise of well-known designers, as well as traditional knitters. The result is this book. I hope it will inspire and encourage home knitters everywhere, and that these patterns will become favorites to knit—and to wear.

Cables

Knitters have always stretched their imagination and creativeness to adorn their work with either color or texture—or both. The earliest knitters relied mostly on different colored dyes to decorate their work, but by, perhaps, the thirteenth century the plaited and braided girdles worn at that time started to inspire knitters to copy the braid effect in their knitting.

By the eighteenth century patterned stockings were part of the traditional dress in Austria and Bavaria. Exquisitely knitted in fine cream wool, they are intricately decorated with lattice and cable patterns and covered with elaborate twists. Unlike the true cables we know now, where several stitches are moved in position across the work, these stitch patterns often used a twist of one stitch, so no cable needle was required. This made the patterns, although very intricate, quicker to work.

Cable patterns were also used to decorate the otherwise plain-colored kilt hose, which have been worn by the Scots since the mid-nineteenth century. Knitted in cream wool, these became quite complex, sometimes with a patterned turnover with scalloped edges and openwork cables on the legs. These are still worn, as are Argyle stockings, with Highland dress and in Scots regiments, where they are part of the uniform of Highland dancers and pipe bands.

Rope or cable patterns were also often used in the fishermen's jerseys and guernseys (or ganseys) from the coastal villages of England and Scotland. They feature among the textured patterns, but on these sweaters they are used as one of a large variety of plain and purl and openwork patterns. The cables all have names, such as Coil of Rope, which link them to the sea and the lives of the fishermen. (Read more about these patterns in the introduction to Gansey Stitch Patterns on page 58.)

We now associate the use of cables most strongly with the knitters of the Aran Islands, off the west coast of Ireland. The first Aran sweater that we would recognize as such was discovered in Dublin in 1936 and was mentioned in *Mary Thomas's Book of Knitting Patterns*, first published in 1938 and reissued in 1943. Since then traditional Aran sweaters have become enduringly popular, and a great number of myths about the origin and meaning of the patterns have grown up.

Knitting these garments provided employment for men and women when times were hard. For this reason, knitters were happy to work these cabled sweaters, although it is very doubtful that the knitters on the Aran Islands had made and worn them as part of their own traditional dress. It is now thought that the fishermen of Aran would have originally worn the navy blue ganseys, which feature cable stitches as part of their design.

Over the years, Aran knitting has developed a character of its own. Usually worked in the thicker undyed wool, it differs in construction and pattern from the older navy blue ganseys. The Aran stitch patterns, by contrast, are usually heavily embossed, and this texture has the advantage of increasing the thickness and therefore the warmth of the garment.

Cable knitting has a long and complex history, but the technique is much loved by today's knitters.

Cable & Seed Stitch Denim Socks

These socks, designed for us by Debbie Abrahams, have a cable with an odd number of stitches; there is a purl stitch in the middle to offer a challenge to the knitter, and the cables are set between panels of seed stitch. The pretty cuff, which gives a feminine look, conceals the ribbing that helps to hold up the sock. Denim cotton yarn is hardwearing and lends itself to textured stitches. As it is washed and worn, the indigo dye will fade, giving the cables a three-dimensional look; the shrinkage in the first wash has been taken into account here.

✳ MATERIALS

Yarn

Rowan Denim (100% cotton, 102 yards/ 92m): 5 x 50g (1¾oz) balls, shade 229 Memphis

Needles

One pair U.S. size 4/3.5mm needles (for casting on)

Set of four double-pointed needles U.S. size 4/3.5mm

Set of four double-pointed needles U.S. size 3/3.25mm

One cable needle

Special Abbreviation

c7b Slip next 4 sts onto a cable needle and hold at the back, k next 3 sts from left-hand needle, slip 4th st on cable needle back onto left-hand needle and k that first, then k rem 3 sts from cable needle.

✳ MEASUREMENTS

To fit 9–9½-inch/23–24cm foot.

Length of leg from bottom of heel (cuff turned over): 13 inches/33cm.

Gauge

Denim is a unique yarn that needs to be washed at a high temperature after it has been knitted to shrink the fabric in length; this is taken into account in the pattern. Before washing 23 sts and 30 rows measure 4 inches/10cm over St st using size 3/3.25mm needles (or size needed to obtain correct gauge).

After washing 23 sts and 34 rows measure 4 inches/10cm over St st using size 3/3.25mm needles (or size needed to obtain correct gauge).

CUFF

Using pair of larger needles cast on 98 sts.

Next row (RS) Knit.

Next row *K7 (pass the second stitch on the right-hand needle over the first, as if for binding off) four times; rep from * 13 more times. *42 sts.*

Next row Knit.

Knit sts onto three double-pointed larger-size needles, working 14 sts onto each needle. Join into a round, taking care not to twist sts and place a marker at first st.

Knit 19 rounds.

Change to smaller double-pointed needles.

Next round (fold line) Purl.

Next round Knit.

The reverse stockinette-stitch side of the fabric will fold back and become the right side of the cuff.

Work 18 rounds in k1, p1 rib.

Keep beg of round marked, and rearrange sts as follows:

Knit first 2 sts that are on first needle onto the third needle. There are now 16 sts on the third needle.

Knit rem 12 sts on first needle and first 2 sts from second needle.

Knit rem 12 sts on second needle and first 2 sts from third needle.

Knit rem 12 sts on third needle.

You now have 14 sts on each needle.

Place a second marker at the new beginning of the round (keeping the original marker).

Next round P1, k1, p1, *inc k-wise into next 3 sts, (k1, p1) twice; rep from * until 4 sts remain; inc k-wise into next 3 sts, k1.

You now have 20 sts on each needle.

LEG

Keeping sts in position on needles as set, cont as follows:

Round 1 K1, p1, k1, (k3, p1, k4, p1, k1) 5 times, k3, p1, k3.

Round 2 P1, k1, p1, (k3, p1, k3, p1, k1, p1) 5 times, k3, p1, k3.

Rounds 3 and 4 Rep rounds 1 and 2.

Round 5 (K1, p1, k1, c7b) 6 times.

Round 6 As round 2.

Rounds 7–16 Rep rounds 1 and 2 5 times.

Rounds 17–64 Rep rounds 5–16 4 times.

Rounds 65–69 Rep rounds 5–9.

Round 70 First needle: p1, k1, p1, (k2tog) 3 times, (k1, p1) twice, k3, p1, k3. *17 sts*. Second needle: (p1, k1, p1, k3, p1, k3) twice. *20 sts*. Third needle: *p1, k1, p1, (k2tog) 3 times, k1. Rep from * once more. *14 sts*.

Round 71 First needle: k1, p1, k6, p1, k4, p1, k3; second needle: (k1, p1, k4, p1, k3) twice; third needle: k1, p1, k6, p1, k3, leaving 2 sts unworked. Slip these 2 sts onto the

beg of the first needle.

The sts are now as follows: first needle 19 sts; second needle 20 sts; third needle 12 sts; the beg of the round marked by the first marker has been reached.

HEEL

K2, p1, k1, p1, k5 across the first 10 sts of the next round onto the third needle.

Slip the rem 9 sts from the first needle and 2 sts from the beginning of the third needle onto the second needle; these are the sts for the instep. There are now 31 sts on the second needle and 20 sts on the other needles. Leave the 31 sts on the second needle or holder for the instep and cont working on the 20 sts of the heel.

Heel flap:

Turn and work back and forth in rows for the heel flap.

Next row (WS) Sl 1 p-wise, (p5, k1) twice, p1, k1, p5.

Next row (RS) Sl 1 k-wise, (k5, p1) twice, k1, p1, k5.

Rep the last 2 rows 12 more times, ending with a RS row.

Turn heel:

Row 1 (WS) P12, p2tog, p1, turn, leaving rem 5 sts unworked.

Row 2 (RS) Sl 1, k5, ssk, k1, turn, leaving rem 5 sts unworked.

Row 3 Sl 1, p6, p2tog, p1, turn, leaving rem 3 sts unworked.

Row 4 Sl 1, k7, ssk, k1, turn, leaving rem 3 sts unworked.

Row 5 Sl 1, p8, p2tog, p1, turn, leaving rem st unworked.

Row 6 Sl 1, k9, ssk, k1, turn, leaving rem st unworked.

Row 7 Sl 1, p10, p2tog, turn.

Row 8 Sl 1, k10, ssk. *12 sts*.

Do not break off yarn.

GUSSET

With RS of the heel flap facing, pick up and k 14 sts along first side of heel flap with first needle, k across 31 sts instep sts on second needle as follows: *k1, p1, (k3, p1) twice, rep from * twice more, k1. Pick up and k 14 sts along second side of heel flap, then k first 6 sts of heel flap onto same needle.

The sts are now as follows: first needle 20 sts; second needle 31 sts; third needle 20 sts.

Cont working in rounds.

Round 1 First needle: k to last 3 sts, k2tog, k1; second needle: p1, (k4, p1) 6 times; third needle: k1, ssk, k rem sts. 19 sts on first and third needles.

Round 2 First needle: k19; second needle: k1, p1, (k3, p1) twice, k1, (p1, k3) twice, p1, k1, (p1, k3) twice, p1, k1; third needle: k19.

Round 3 First needle: k to last 3 sts, k2tog, k1; 2nd needle: p1, (k4, p1) 6 times; third needle: k1, ssk, knit rem sts. 18 sts on first and third needles.

Round 4 First needle: k18; second needle: k1, p1, (k3, p1) twice, k1, (p1, k3) twice, p1, k1, (p1, k3) twice, p1, k1; third needle: k18.

Round 5 First needle: k to last 3 sts, k2tog, k1; second needle: p1, k1, (c7b, k1, p1, k1) twice, c7b, k1, p1; third needle: k1, ssk, k rem sts. 17 sts on first and third needles.

Round 6 First needle: k17; second needle: k1, p1, (k3, p1) twice, k1, (p1, k3) twice, p1, k1, (p1, k3) twice, p1, k1; third needle: k17.

Round 7 First needle: k to last 3 sts, k2tog, k1; second needle: p1, (k4, p1) 6 times; third needle: k1, ssk, k rem sts. 16 sts on first and third needles.

Round 8 First needle: k16; second needle: k1, p1, (k3, p1) twice, k1, (p1, k3) twice, p1, k1, (p1, k3) twice, p1, k1; third needle: k16.

Round 9 First needle: k to last 3 sts, k2tog, k1; second needle: p1, (k4, p1) 6 times; third needle: k1, ssk, k rem sts. 15 sts on first and third needles.

Round 10 First needle: k15; second needle: k1, p1, (k3, p1) twice, k1,

(p1, k3) twice, p1, k1, (p1, k3) twice, p1, k1; third needle: k15.

Round 11 First needle: k to last 3 sts, k2tog, k1; second needle: p1, (k4, p1) 6 times; third needle: k1, ssk, k rem sts. 14 sts on first and third needles.

Round 12 First needle: k14; second needle: k1, p1, (k3, p1) twice, k1, (p1, k3) twice, p1, k1, (p1, k3) twice, p1, k1; third needle: k14.

Round 13 First needle: k to last 3 sts, k2tog, k1; second needle: p1, (k4, p1) 6 times; third needle: k1, ssk, k rem sts. 13 sts on first and third needles.

Round 14 First needle: k13; second needle: k1, p1, (k3, p1) twice, k1, (p1, k3) twice, p1, k1, (p1, k3) twice, p1, k1; third needle: k13.

Round 15 First needle: k to last 3 sts, k2tog, k1; second needle: p1, (k4, p1) 6 times; third needle: k1, ssk, k rem sts. 12 sts on first and third needles.

Round 16 First needle: k12; second needle: k1, p1, (k3, p1) twice, k1, (p1, k3) twice, p1, k1, (p1, k3) twice, p1, k1; third needle: k12.

Round 17 First needle: k to last 3 sts, k2tog, k1; second needle: p1, k1, (c7b, k1, p1, k1) twice, c7b, k1, p1; third needle: k1, ssk, k rem sts. 11 sts on first and third needles.

Round 18 First needle: k11; second needle: k1, p1, (k3, p1) twice, k1,

(p1, k3) twice, p1, k1, (p1, k3) twice, p1, k1; third needle: k11.

Round 19 First needle: k to last 3 sts, k2tog, k1; second needle: p1, (k4, p1) 6 times; third needle: k1, ssk, k rem sts. 10 sts on first and third needles.

Round 20 First needle: k10; second needle: k1, p1, (k3, p1) twice, k1, (p1, k3) twice, p1, k1, (p1, k3) twice, p1, k1; third needle: k10.
The sts are now arranged as follows: first needle 10 sts; second needle 31 sts; third needle 10 sts.

FOOT

Round 1 First needle: k10; second needle: p1, (k4, p1) 6 times; third needle: k10.

Round 2 First needle: k10; second needle: k1, p1, (k3, p1) twice, k1, (p1, k3) twice, p1, k1, (p1, k3) twice, p1, k1; third needle: k10.

Rounds 3–8 Rep rounds 1 and 2, 3 times.

Round 9 First needle: k10; second needle: p1, k1, (c7b, k1, p1, k1) twice, c7b, k1, p1; third needle: k10.

Round 10 As round 2.

Rounds 11 and 12 Rep rounds 1 and 2.

Rounds 13–20 Rep rounds 1–8.
Rep rounds 9–20 until foot measures 2 inches/5cm less than the desired length, finishing after completing a round 12.

Next round (decrease) First needle: k10; second needle: (k2tog) 4 times, k2, p1, k1, (k2tog) 3 times, k2, p1, k1, (k2tog) 3 times, k1, k2tog (20 sts); third needle: k10.

SHAPE TOE

Round 1 First needle: k to last 3 sts, k2tog, k1; second needle: k1, ssk, k to last 3 sts, k2tog, k1; third needle: k1, ssk, k rem sts.
Round 2 Knit.
Rounds 3–8 Rep rounds 1 and 2, 3 times. *24 sts.*
Round 9 As round 1. *20 sts.*
K 5 sts from first needle onto third needle. There are now 10 sts on each of the two rem needles.
Graft (see page 142) or bind off sts tog on the WS.

Work a second sock in the same way.

FINISHING

Wash the socks in the washing machine on a hot wash. Reshape and dry flat away from direct heat.
Note Dye loss will occur, so wash separately or with jeans or other dark colors.

Wellington Boot Socks

A double-knitting weight of a Scottish tweed wool is an ideal yarn for these chunky socks, which can be worn by men and women. The socks are worked with an auto heel, which uses short rows to form the heel, and a flat toe; a cable down the side adds an element of pattern. This shaping is based on a vintage pattern for wading-boot socks for fishermen, and is reminiscent of socks worn at sea in the 1930s and 1940s. Quick to knit and just the thing to wear on winter walks or for gardening, these socks will keep your feet toasty on the coldest of days.

✳ MATERIALS

Yarn

Rowan Scottish Tweed DK (100% pure wool, 123 yards/113m): 4 x 50g (1¾oz) balls, shade 00008 Herring

Needles

Set of four double-pointed needles U.S. size 5/3.75mm

One cable needle

Special Abbreviation

c6b Slip the next 3 sts onto a cable needle and hold back of work, k the next 3 sts, k3 from cable needle.

✳ MEASUREMENTS

To fit 9½ [10½]-inch/24 [27]cm foot (adjustable).

Length of leg from bottom of heel (cuff folded): 16½ inches/42cm.

Gauge

22 sts and 28 rows measure 4 inches/10cm using size 5/3.75mm needles (or size needed to obtain correct gauge).

Cast on 56 [64] sts and join, being careful not to twist sts. Work in k2, p2 rib for 5 inches/13cm, inc to 60 [68] sts on last round.

CABLE PATTERN

Round 1 K10 [12], p2, k6, p2, k20 [24], p2, k6, p2, k10 [12].
Rep this round 5 more times.
Round 7 K10 [12], p2, c6b, p2, k20 [24], p2, c6b, p2, k10 [12].
Round 8 As Round 1.
Rep these 8 rounds twice more.
1st dec round K8 [10], k2tog, p2, k6, p2, k2tog, k16 [20], k2tog tbl, p2, k6,

p2, k2tog tbl, k8 [10].
Cont even in patt as set for 8 rounds.
2nd dec round K7 [9], k2tog, p2, k6, p2, k2tog, k14 [18], k2tog tbl, p2, k6, p2, k2tog tbl, k7 [9].
Cont even in patt as set for 8 rounds.
3rd dec round K6 [8], k2tog, p2, k6, p2, k2tog, k12 [16], k2tog tbl, p2, k6, p2, k2tog tbl, k6 [8].
Cont in patt as set on these 48 [56] sts until work measures 15¾ inches/40cm.

ANKLE RIBBING

Next round Work first and last 5 sts in k1, p1 rib and k the rest.
Work even for 11 more rounds.
Next round Work first and last 7 sts in k1, p1 rib and k the rest.
Work even for 11 more rounds.
Next round Work first and last 9 sts in k1, p1 rib and k the rest.
Work even for 11 more rounds, leaving the last 12 [14] sts on the last round unworked.

HEEL & INSTEP

Slip first and last 12 [14] sts onto one needle for heel. Divide the other sts onto two needles and leave for instep. Shape heel as follows:
Row 1 K23 [27], turn.
Row 2 P22 [26], turn.
Row 3 K21 [25], turn.
Row 4 P20 [24], turn.

Cont in this way, working 1 st fewer on every row until the row "P10, turn" has been worked.

Next row K10, pick up loop lying below next st and k it tog with next st, turn.

Next row P11, pick up loop lying below next st and p it tog with next st, turn.

Cont in this way, working 1 st more on every row until all 24 [28] sts are on needle.

Place a colored marker at this point.

Next row K12 [14]. Heel completed.

Slip all instep sts onto one needle. 12 [14] sts on first needle, 24 [28] sts on second needle, and 12 [14] sts on third needle.

Working in rounds, cont in St st until work measures 7 [8] inches/ 18 [20]cm or 2 inches/5cm less than desired total length.

SHAPE TOE

Round 1 First needle: k to last 3 sts, k2tog, k1; 2nd needle: k1, ssk, k to last 3 sts, k2tog, k1; 3rd needle: k1, ssk, k to end.

Round 2 Knit.

Rep these 2 rounds until 20 [24] sts rem. K sts of first needle onto end of third needle. Graft (see page 142) or bind off together the two sets of sts. Make another sock in the same way.

FINISHING

Block or press carefully (see page 143).

Cable & Fancy Stitch Socks

These socks have a pretty cable and twist stitch that stems from a vintage pattern and is interesting to knit. The cable pattern is prettily set off by the narrower—slightly openwork—patterns in between. The socks are knitted on two needles and shaped to fit the leg nicely. The original pattern was designed as a sports sock, but we have used a luxurious, soft cashmere blend, making the socks gorgeous to knit and to wear. The finished result is a classic that somehow manages to be both old-fashioned and up-to-date.

✳ MATERIALS

Yarn

Debbie Bliss Baby Cashmerino
(55% merino wool, 33% microfiber,
12% cashmere; approx 114 yards/
125m): 5 x 50g (approx 1¼ oz) balls,
shade 203 Teal

Needles

One pair U.S. size 2/2.75mm needles
One pair U.S. size 3/3mm needles
One cable needle

Special Abbreviations

tw3 *Pass third st on left-hand needle over*
the first and second sts, letting the loop
drop off needle, then k1, yo, k1.
c6 *Slip next 3 sts onto a cable needle and*
leave at back of work, k the next 3 sts,
then k the 3 sts from cable needle.

✳ MEASUREMENTS

To fit 8½–9-inch/22–23cm foot.
Length of leg from bottom of heel:
12 inches/31cm.

Gauge

28 sts and 40 rows measure 4 inches/10cm
using size 2/2.75mm needles (or size
needed to obtain correct gauge). Note:
These socks were knitted with metric
needles; if you have trouble achieving the
correct gauge, try using metric needles.

Using larger needles, cast on 93 sts.
Change to smaller needles.

Row 1 K1, (p1, k1) to end.

Row 2 P1, (k1, p1) to end.

Rep these 2 rows 3 more times.

PATTERN

Row 1 K2, (p2, k3, p2, k6, p2, k3, p2, k3) to end, but finish last rep with k2.

Row 2 P2, (k2, p3, k2, p6, k2, p3, k2, p3) to end, but finish last rep with p2.

Row 3 K2, (p2, tw3, p2, k6, p2, tw3, p2, k3) to end, but finish last rep with k2.

Row 4 As row 2.

Row 5 As row 1.

Row 6 As row 2.

Row 7 K2, (p2, tw3, p2, c6, p2, tw3, p2, k3) to end, but finish last rep with k2.

Row 8 As row 2.

These 8 rows form the pattern.

Rep them 11 more times, then keeping continuity of patt, shape as follows: Dec 1 st at each end of next row and every foll 6th row until 83 sts rem (3 patt repeats in all). Work 7 rows even. Break off yarn and beg instep as follows.

INSTEP

Next row Slip first 21 sts onto a thread or stitch holder and leave for heel. Join yarn to next st and work in patt over the next 41 sts. Turn,

then slip remaining 21 sts onto another thread or stitch holder. Work 40 rows in patt on the 41 instep sts.

Next row (WS) P4, p2tog, p6, p2tog (p3, p2tog) 3 times, p6, p2tog, p4. Work 2 rows St st.

SHAPE TOE

Cont in St st work as follows:
Row 1 K2, sl 1, skp to last 4 sts, k2tog, k2.
Row 2 Purl.
Rep these 2 rows until 15 sts rem; leave these sts on a spare needle.

HEEL

Slip the 2 sets of heel sts onto a smaller needle, placing outer edges of work in center to form back seam, then with RS facing, join yarn.
Next row (K9, k2tog) 3 times, k to end.
Beg with a p row, work 20 rows in st st on these 39 sts, finishing with a k row. Now turn heel as follows:
Row 1 P27, p2tog, turn.
Row 2 K13, skp, turn.
Row 3 P13, p2tog, turn.
Rep rows 2 and 3 until there are 13 sts on needle, slip them onto the other needle.
With RS of work facing, join yarn to first row of heel at right-hand

side and pick up and k 16 sts along the row ends. K the 13 sts left on needle, then pick up and k 16 sts along other side of heel.

SOLE

Now work on these 45 sts for sole section as follows:
Row 1 Purl.
Row 2 Knit.
Row 3 Purl.
Row 4 K2, skp, k to last 4 sts, k2tog, k2.
Row 5 Purl.
Rep rows 2–5 4 more times. Work 20 rows in st st on the remaining 35 sts to beg of toe shaping, ending with a p row.
Now shape toe as given above, then graft (see page 142) or bind off the two sets of 15 sts tog.

Make another sock in the same way.

FINISHING

Join leg and foot seams. Block or press carefully (see page 143).

Aran Socks

Knitted in the round, these chunky socks are decorated down the front with a traditional Aran cable, which forms large diamond panels with seed stitch in the center. Some say the diamonds represent the shape of the fishing-net mesh, and seed stitch is sometimes called "Poor Man's Wealth." Whatever the myths that have arisen over the years, these patterns show what can be achieved with simple knit and purl stitches. These are cozy indoor socks with a wide leg that will slouch down into wrinkles and are ideal for wearing while curled up on the sofa in front of the fire.

✳ MATERIALS

Yarn

Rowan pure wool Aran (100% super-wash wool, 186 yards/170m): 2 x 100g (3½oz) balls, shade 670 Ivory

Needles

Set of four double-pointed needles U.S. size 7/4.5mm

One cable needle

Special Abbreviations

tw2 *K into second then into first st and slip both off needle together.*

c5f *Slip next 3 sts onto cable needle and hold at front, k2, slip purl st from cable needle back onto left-hand needle and purl it, k2 from cable needle.*

t3b *Slip next st onto cable needle and hold at back, k2, then p st from cable needle.*

t3f *Slip 2 sts onto cable needle and hold at front, p1, k2 from cable needle.*

✳ MEASUREMENTS

To fit 9 [10]-inch/23 [25.5]cm foot (adjustable).

Length of leg from bottom of heel: 15 inches/38cm.

Note: *This sock is intended to be a loose fit on the leg and to slouch down.*

Gauge

22 sts and 28 rows measure 4 inches/10cm using size 7/4.5mm needles (or size needed to obtain correct gauge).

Cast on 76 sts and join, being careful not to twist sts.

Beginning and ending round with k1, work k2, p2 ribbing for 1 inch/2.5cm, dec 1 st in middle of last round. *75 sts.*

Keeping sts at back of leg in rib, place and work central cable panel as follows:

Set up round Rib 26, cable panel of 23 sts: p1, k2, p6, k2, p1, k2, p6, k2, p1; rib 26.

CABLE PANEL

Round 1 P1, k2, p6, c5f, p6, k2, p1.
Round 2 P1, k2, p6, k2, p1, k2, p6, k2, p1.
Round 3 P1, tw2, p5, t3b, k1, t3f, p5, tw2, p1.
Round 4 P1, k2, p5, k2, p1, k1, p1, k2, p5, k2, p1.
Round 5 P1, k2, p4, t3b, k1, p1, k1, t3f, p4, k2, p1.
Round 6 P1, k2, p4, k2, (p1, k1) twice, p1, k2, p4, k2, p1.
Round 7 P1, tw2, p3, t3b, (k1, p1) twice, k1, t3f, p3, tw2, p1.
Round 8 P1, k2, p3, k2, (p1, k1) 3 times, p1, k2, p3, k2, p1.
Round 9 P1, k2, p2, t3b, (k1, p1) 3 times, k1, t3f, p2, k2, p1.
Round 10 P1, k2, p2, k2, (p1, k1) 4 times, p1, k2, p2, k2, p1.
Round 11 P1, tw2, p2, t3b, (k1, p1)

4 times, k1, t3f, p1, tw2, p1.
Round 12 P1, k2, p1, k2, (p1, k1) 5 times, p1, k2, p1, k2, p1.
Round 13 P1, k2, p1, t3f, (p1, k1) 4 times, p1, t3b, p1, k2, p1.
Round 14 P1, k2, p2, k2, (p1, k1) 4 times, p1, k2, p2, k2, p1.
Round 15 P1, tw2, p2, t3f, (p1, k1) 3 times, p1, t3b, p2, tw2, p1.
Round 16 P1, k2, p3, k2, (p1, k1) 3 times, p1, k2, p3, k2, p1.
Round 17 P1, k2, p3, t3f, (p1, k1) twice, p1, t3b, p3, k2, p1.
Round 18 P1, k2, p4, k2, (p1, k1) twice, p1, k2, p4, k2, p1.
Round 19 P1, tw2, p4, t3f, p1, k1, p1, t3b, p4, tw2, p1.
Round 20 P1, k2, p5, k2, p1, k1, p1, k2, p5, k2, p1.
Round 21 P1, k2, p5, t3f, p1, t3b, p5, k2, p1.
Round 22 P1, k2, p6, k2, p1, k2, p6, k2, p1.

Rep these 22 rounds twice more but working the twisted stitches that outline the cables on every 4th row; i.e. they will not always repeat on the same rows as those numbered above.

HEEL FLAP

(K2tog) 13 times, turn; p13, (p2tog) 13 times. *26 sts.*

These sts will form the heel.

Leave the rem sts on a spare needle or stitch holder for instep.

Row 1 (Sl 1, k1) to end.
Row 2 Sl 1, p to end.
Rep these 2 rows 9 more times.

Turn heel:
Row 1 Sl 1, k16, skp, turn.
Row 2 Sl 1, p8, p2tog, turn.
Row 3 Sl 1, k8, skp, turn.
Rep rows 2 and 3 until all sts have been worked, ending on a purl row.
Knit 1 row across all 10 sts.

GUSSETS

Pick up sts for the gussets:
On same needle as heel sts, pick up and k 11 sts along edge of heel flap. Work in patt across instep sts with separate needle, pick up and k 11 sts along other edge of heel flap, and on same needle k 5 to center of heel. *55 sts.*

Shape gussets:
Next round First needle: k to last 3 sts, k2tog, k1; second needle: patt across instep; third needle: k1, skp, k to end.

Next round Work 1 round even.
Rep these 2 rounds until 47 sts remain, then dec at end of first needle only.

INSTEP

Cont working cable patt over center portion of sts until a complete diamond has been worked, then cont in St st until sock measures 6½ [7½] inches/16.5 [19]cm from back of heel (or 2 inches/5cm less than desired length). Divide sts over the needles so that first needle has 11 sts, second needle has 23 sts, and third needle has 12 sts.

DECREASE FOR TOE

Round 1 First needle: k to last 3 sts, k2tog, k1; second needle: k1, skp, k to last 3 sts, k2tog, k1; third needle: k1, skp, k to end.
Round 2 Knit.
Rep these 2 rounds until 18 sts remain. Divide these sts onto two needles and graft (see page 142) or bind off tog on WS.

Make another sock in the same way.

FINISHING

Block or press carefully (see page 143).

Traditional Kilt Hose

Traditional kilt hose are the perfect accompaniment to Highland dress, but they can be worn as warm socks on many other occasions. They have a turnover cuff below the knee, and the cuff on this pair is decorated with the chain cable pattern, a very old, traditional pattern related to honeycomb stitch. The wool used here is from one of the British sheep breeds, Bluefaced Leicester, which has an extremely fine fleece, giving this double-knitting-weight wool a lovely handle and luster. The socks are knitted on four needles, from the cuff down, and the natural cream wool shows up the stitch patterns to great advantage.

✳ MATERIALS

Yarn

Rowan British Sheep Breeds DK undyed
(100% British wool, 131 yards/120m):
5 x 50g (1¾oz) balls, shade 780
Bluefaced Leicester

Needles

Set of four double-pointed needles
U.S. size 6/4mm
One cable needle

Special Abbreviations

c4b *Place next 2 sts on cable needle and*
leave at back of work, k2, then k2
from cable needle.

c4f *Place next 2 sts on cable needle and*
leave at front of work, k2, then k2
from cable needle.

✳ MEASUREMENTS

To fit 10 [10½, 11]-inch/25 [27, 28]cm
foot (adjustable).

Length of leg from bottom of heel (cuff
folded): 17 inches/43cm.

Gauge

24 sts and 32 rows measure 4 inches/10cm
using size 6/4mm needles (or size needed
to obtain correct gauge).

Cast on 80 sts and divide them over three needles. Join, being careful not to twist sts.
Work 5 rows in k1, p1 rib.

CABLE PATTERN

Round 1 (P2, k8) to end.
Round 2 (P2, c4b, c4f) to end.
Rounds 3–6 As round 1.
Round 7 (P2, c4f, c4b) to end.
Round 8 As round 1.
Rep rounds 1–8 twice more.

Cont in k1, p1 rib until work measures 7 inches/18cm from beg. Turn work inside out.

Cont in rib patt for leg:
Round 1 (P1, k1, p1, k1, p1, k5) to end.
Round 2 (P5, k5) to end.
Rep these 2 rounds until work measures 2 inches/5cm then K2tog tbl at beg of every St st panel.
Work even for 4 inches/10cm on these 72 sts then k2tog at end of every knit panel.
Work even on these 64 sts until work measures 18 inches/45cm (or desired length).
Patt 13, turn, p13 then p16 from end of previous round onto same needle (29 sts for heel).
Divide rem 36 sts over two needles and leave for instep.

HEEL

Work 26 rows in St st, always slipping first st.

Turn heel:
Next row Sl 1, k17, turn.
Next row Sl 1, p6, turn.
Next row Sl 1, k5, k2tog, k1, turn.
Next row Sl 1, p6, p2tog, p1, turn.
Next row Sl 1, k7, k2tog, k1, turn.
Cont in this way, working 1 more st before decs until the row "Sl 1, p14, p2tog, p1" has been worked.
Next row Sl 1, k15, k2tog.
Next row Sl 1, p15, p2tog.
Next row Sl 1, k8. Heel is completed and 8 sts rem unworked on left needle.

FOOT

Slip all instep sts onto one needle. Using a spare needle, k 8 sts from heel, pick up and k 14 sts along side of heel. Using second needle, patt 36 sts from instep; using third needle, pick up and k 14 sts along other side of heel. K rem 9 sts.
Round 1 K sts from first and third needles, patt sts from second needle.
Round 2 First needle: patt to last 3 sts, k2tog, k1; second needle: work in patt; third needle: k1, k2tog tbl, k to end.
Rep these 2 rounds until there are 64 sts then work as set until work measures 8 [8½, 9] inches/20 [22, 23]cm

from back of heel. Arrange sts so that there are 15 on first needle, 33 on second needle, and 16 on third needle.

Next round K15, k1, k2tog tbl, k27, k2tog, k1, k16.

Next round Knit.

Next round K to last 3 sts of first needle, k2tog, k1; second needle: k1, k2tog tbl, k to last 3 sts, k2tog, k1; third needle: k1, k2tog tbl, k to end. Rep last 2 rounds until there are 22 sts. Rearrange sts on 2 needles and graft (see page 142) or bind off tog on the WS.

Make another sock in the same way.

FINISHING

Block or press carefully (see page 143).

Stripes & Multicolor

Some of the earliest pieces of knitting are medieval Egyptian socks. These do not have purl (or pearl) stitches and suggest that tubular knitting, using only a knit stitch, was used first. The advantage of working in knit stitches in the round is that the right side of the work is always facing you, making the working of multicolored patterns easier to do.

The natural colors of the sheep, and therefore the yarn—which could range through very dark brown and mid brown to different shades of fawn and gray—provided color. Early dyes were confined to vegetable and plant dyes, the most common being madder red and indigo blue. Striped work was being made from the fourth or fifth century in Egypt in a precursor of knitting called nailbinding. Stripes are still popular today, either on their own or combined with small patterns.

Real knitting developed in Islamic Egypt from the seventh century, and a fragment from that time has been found with an elaborate pattern in red and yellow silk. There are other early examples in blue and white cotton made in Egypt around the twelfth century, now in the Textile Museum at Washington, D.C.; we have paid homage to one of these in our Egyptian socks (see page 38). All these early socks were knitted from the toe up, like our Egyptian socks and Turkish socks (see page 46).

Some early knitting is surprisingly colorful, with up to six dyed colors of cotton or wool, and geometrical patterns like chevrons and diamonds, as well as motifs representing plants and animals, similar to those often found in old carpets. Multicolored coin purses, gloves, and socks, all with elaborate patterns, are found in Albania, Turkey, Greece, and Switzerland from medieval times to the near-present day, often as part of traditional dress. Turkey is home to some of the most colorful socks, knitted from the toe up on five needles, with a different pattern on the sole. The triangular toe and the heel—called a peasant heel—are the same shape, with the heel stitches picked up and worked in the opposite direction. Three or four colors or more could be used in any one round, so the knitter had to be very skillful. Our pattern has only two colors in a round, but is a typical Turkish design.

Glove and stocking knitting in Britain flourished in the borders of Scotland, and the patterns were often small and geometric, worked in two colors, like the distinctive patterns from Sanquhar. The Shetland Islands produced their own unique, more colorful patterns (see page 74).

With the renewed interest in knitting in the 1970s and 1980s, many designers set up their own knitwear businesses, and many supplied my shop. One of these was Sasha Kagan, who is now known internationally and primarily works in the intarsia method. Her Intarsia Flower Socks (page 34) are a pretty, modern interpretation of an age-old craft.

Sasha Kagan's Intarsia Flower Socks

Sasha Kagan set up her knitwear business in 1972, two years after The Scottish Merchant opened in Covent Garden, London, and the shop was one of her first outlets. Since then she has gone from strength to strength; she has published many books on knitting and has become an internationally known knitwear designer with garments in London's Victoria and Albert Museum. Sasha is one of the foremost designers working with the intarsia technique and is known for her use of color, pattern, and texture. She designed these socks especially for this book— and called them Madeline's Socks—using yarns that have a small proportion of a harder-wearing fiber to produce socks that are both pretty and practical.

 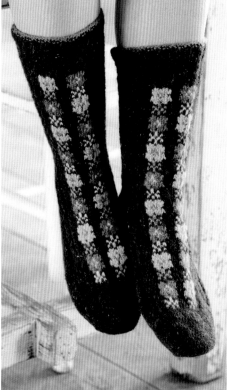 

✱ MATERIALS

Yarn

Rowan Felted Tweed (50% merino wool,
    25% alpaca, 25% viscose, approx
    191 yards/175m):

2 x 50g (1¾oz) balls, shade 145 Treacle (B)

Rowan Cashsoft DK (57% extra-fine
    merino, 33% acrylic microfiber,
    10% cashmere, 142 yards/130m):

1 x 50g (1¾oz) ball, shade 00529
    Admiral (A)

1 x 50g (1¾oz) ball, shade 00522
    Cashew (C)

1 x 50g (1¾ oz) ball, shade 00509 Lime (D)

1 x 50g (1¾ oz) ball, shade 00520 Bloom (E)

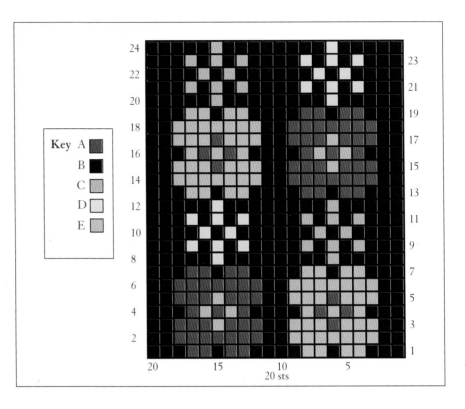

Needles

One pair U.S. size 2/2.75mm needles

Special Abbreviation

tw2 K into second st on left-hand needle,
stretch the st just made slightly, then k into
back of first st and slip both sts off needles.

✱ MEASUREMENTS

To fit 9 [10]-inch/23 [25.5]cm foot.
Length of leg from bottom of heel:
    11½ inches/29cm.

Gauge

28 sts and 38 rows measure 4 inches/10cm
over St st using size 2/2.75mm needles (or
size needed to obtain correct gauge).

SPECIAL INSTRUCTIONS

The chart panel is knitted using the intarsia method (see page 141). For this, each separate block of color is worked using a separate length of yarn. Weave background yarn B along behind blocks, catching it in on every other stitch.

MOCK CABLE RIB PATTERN

Row 1 (P2, tw2) rep to last 2 sts, p2.
Row 2 (K2, p2) to last 2 sts, k2.
Row 3 (P2, k2) to last 2 sts, p2.
Row 4 As Row 2.

These 4 rows form the pattern.

Using yarn A cast on 74 sts.
Work 1 row mock cable rib starting with p2.
Change to yarn B and work 2 inches/ 5cm mock cable rib starting with p2. Work 26 sts mock cable rib with yarn B, k1, then work across 20 sts of chart foll the chart from right to left for knit rows and left to right for purl rows. Then k1, and work 26 sts of mock cable rib in yarn B. Cont as set until foot measures approx 6½ inches/16.5cm, ending after row 7 or 19 of chart in order to complete a flower motif.

Divide for heel and instep:

Next row Patt 55 sts, turn, leaving 19 sts on a stitch holder.

Next row Patt 36 sts, turn, leaving 19 sts on a stitch holder.

Cont on these 36 sts in patt for 48 [56] rows.

HEEL FLAP

Leave these stitches on a spare needle. With RS facing slip sts from both holders onto one needle with back of leg seam at center. Work 20 rows mock cable rib on 38 sts.

Turn heel:

Row 1 K28, skp, turn.

Row 2 P19, p2tog, turn.

Row 3 K19, skp, turn.

Row 4 As row 2.

Rep last 2 rows until 20 sts rem, ending with a p row, then onto same needle, pick up and p 16 sts along side of heel flap. *36 sts*.

Next row K to end, then pick up and k 16 sts along other side of heel flap. *52 sts*.

Next row Purl.

Now cont in St st and shape instep as follows:

Row 1 K1, skp, k to last 3 sts, k2tog, k1.

Row 2 K1, p to last st, k1.

Rep last 2 rows until 36 sts remain, then cont in St st until foot section measures same as top section, ending with a WS row.

Next row K to end, then k across 36 sts on spare needle. *72 sts*.

Next row Purl.

SHAPE TOE:

Row 1 (K1, k2tog, k30, k2tog, k1) twice.

Row 2 and every alt row Purl.

Row 3 (K1, k2tog, k28, k2tog, k1) twice.

Row 5 (K1, k2tog, k26, k2tog, k1) twice.

Cont to dec in this way on alt rows until 28 sts remain, ending with a WS row. Then slip first 14 sts onto a spare needle, fold work in half with RS facing, and graft sts tog (see page 142).

Make another sock in the same way.

FINISHING

Darn loose ends back into their own color. Join the seams at the side of the foot and at back of leg (see page 143).

Block or press carefully (see page 143).

Egyptian Socks

Patterned Egyptian socks are among the oldest pieces of knitting to have survived to this day, and the striking pattern featured here is based on a sock found in northern Egypt that dates from between the eleventh and fourteenth centuries. Made from natural undyed cotton and dark indigo-blue cotton, it was knitted in the round, from the toe up, in two-color stranded knitting. The original stocking, in the Textile Museum in Washington, D.C., has been the subject of much research. Our version copies some of the patterns, but is shorter, and has a modern shaping to the toe and heel. Knitted in the round, like the original, and using a 4-ply cotton yarn, this pattern transforms a museum piece into a pretty, wearable design for today.

✳ MATERIALS

Yarn

Rowan Siena 4-ply (100% cotton,
153 yards/140m):
2 x 50g (1¾oz) balls, shade 672 Mariner (A)
1 x 50g (1¾oz) ball, shade 652 Cream (B)

Needles

Set of four double-pointed needles U.S.
size 2/2.75mm
Set of four double-pointed needles U.S.
size 3/3.25mm

✳ MEASUREMENTS

To fit 7½–inch/19cm foot (adjustable).
Length of leg from bottom of heel:
12 inches/31cm.

Gauge

32 stitches and 44 rows measure 4 inches/
10cm using size 2/2.75mm needles (or size
needed to obtain correct gauge).

✳ NOTE

These socks are knitted from the toe up.

Using yarn A, smaller needles, and the "figure 8" method (see page 142), cast on 32 sts: 16 on each of two needles. When cast-on is completed continue on the two needles, working increases as follows:

Round 1 First needle: k1, M1, k to last st, M1, k1; second needle: repeat as for first needle.

Round 2 Knit 1 round even. Rep these 2 rounds until there are 64 sts: 32 on each of two needles.

Divide work over three needles and knit 4 rounds.

STRIPES

Starting with yarn B, and using B and A alternately, work 2 rounds of each color until 3 stripes of B have been completed. Work 2 rounds in A, inc 1 st at each end of second round. *66 sts.*

Length of foot can be adjusted to the desired measurement by working extra stripes here or in A rows between diamond patterns.

DIAMONDS

Using both A and B work the 9 rows of Chart 1. Rep Chart 1 twice more, omitting the first row on the second and third repeats.

Using A, work 4 rounds.

HEEL

When foot is about 2½ inches/6cm less than desired foot size, divide sts for heel. Keep first 33 heel sts on working needle and leave 33 instep sts on a stitch holder.

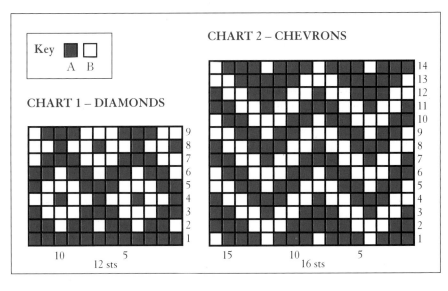

Key ■ □
A B

CHART 2 – CHEVRONS

14
13
12
11
10
9
8
7
6
5
4
3
2
1

15   10   5
16 sts

CHART 1 – DIAMONDS

9
8
7
6
5
4
3
2
1

10   5
12 sts

On the 33 heel sts, work short-row shaping as follows (see page 141):
Row 1 K32, wrap last st, turn.
Row 2 Slip wrapped st, k31, wrap last st, turn.
Cont as for rows 1 and 2, reducing the number of sts worked on each row until you have 14 sts unwrapped in the middle; these form the first part of the heel.

Next row K across the 14 sts to the first unworked and wrapped st. Pick up the wrap, k it tog with the st, wrap the next st, turn. This st has been wrapped twice.
Next row Slip the first double-wrapped st, p across to the first unworked wrapped st. Pick up the wrap, p it tog with the st, turn. Cont in this way, picking up both wraps and knitting or purling them tog with the st. The heel is complete

when all 33 sts have been worked. At the end of the heel shaping, on the first round when all sts are ready to be worked, pick up 1 extra st at both joins between the heel sts and the unworked instep sts to prevent any holes. *68 sts.*

STRIPES

Using yarn B and A alternately, work 2 rounds of each color until 3 stripes of B have been completed. Work 7 rounds in A, inc 4 sts evenly on last round. *72 sts.*

CHEVRONS

Using A and B work the 14 rows of Chart 2.
Cont in stripes, working 4 rounds of A, 2 rounds of B, and 3 rounds of A.

DIAMONDS

Using A and B work the 9 rows of Chart 1 twice, omitting row 1 the second time.

Change to larger needles and work one more repeat of Chart 1, again omitting row 1 of chart as before. Using A work 2 rounds; using B work 2 rounds; using A work 4 rounds.

CHEVRONS

Using A and B yarns, work the 14 rows of Chart 2.
Cont in stripes, working 3 rounds of A, 2 rounds of B, and 2 rounds of A.

RIBBED CUFF

Cont with A, work in k1, p1 rib for 4 rounds. Bind off.
More rounds can be worked if a deeper cuff is desired.

Make another sock in the same way.

FINISHING

Sew in ends. Block or press carefully (see page 143).

Striped Socks

Simple stripes can make an eye-catching pair of socks, and the color combinations you can choose are virtually endless. These are knitted in a wool and cotton blend, which is soft and has the qualities of both natural yarns. If you want to knit in stripes without breaking off your yarn when you change color, the stripes must be narrow, and here they are only two rows wide. There is a good technique to use to avoid a "jog" at the color change, which is noted in the pattern, and makes for a neatly finished sock.

✳ MATERIALS

Yarn

Rowan Wool Cotton (50% merino,
50% cotton, 123 yards/113m):
2 x 50g (1¾oz) balls, shade 930 Riviera (A)
2 x 50g (1¾oz) balls, shade 907 Deepest
Olive (B)

Needles

Set of four double-pointed needles U.S. size
2/3mm
Set of four double pointed needles U.S. size
3/3.25mm

✳ MEASUREMENTS

To fit 9½ [10, 10½]-inch/24 [25, 27]cm foot.
Length of leg from bottom of heel:
12 inches/30cm.

Gauge

24 sts and 33 rows measure 4 inches/10cm
using size 3/3.25mm needles (or size needed
to obtain correct gauge). Note: These socks
were knitted with metric needles; if you
have trouble achieving the correct gauge,
try using metric needles).

✳ NOTE

Changing color while knitting in the round
creates a "jog," or visible join, at the
beginning/end of the round. To prevent this,
knit one round in the new color; then, at the
start of the second round of the new color, slip
the first stitch purlwise and continue knitting.

Using yarn A and smaller needles, cast on 60 sts and join, being careful not to twist sts (20 sts on each of three needles). Work in k2, p2 rib for 3 inches/7.5cm.

Change to larger needles and work in St st and stripe patt knitting 2 rows in B, followed by 2 rows in A alternately, for 4 inches/10cm. Cont in stripe patt, dec as follows:
Next round K2, k2tog, k to last 4 sts, k2tog tbl, k2.
Work 6 rounds even.
Next round K2, k2tog, k to last 4 sts, k2tog tbl, k2.
Cont to dec in this way on every 7th round until 52 sts rem.
Work even until work measures 10¼ inches/26cm.

HEEL

Using yarn B, k13, sl last 13 sts of round onto end of same needle; these 26 sts are for the heel. Divide remainder of sts onto two needles for instep.

Work 19 rows in yarn B in St st on heel sts, slipping first and knitting last st in every row.

Turn heel:
K16, k2tog tbl, turn; p7, p2tog, turn; k8, k2tog tbl, turn; p9, p2tog, turn; cont in this way until all sts are worked onto one needle again. 16 sts remain for heel.
Next row K8 sts to complete heel. Slip all instep sts onto one needle again. Taking another needle, k across remaining 8 heel sts and pick up and k 17 sts from side of heel; with second needle, k across instep sts. With third needle, pick up and k 17 sts from other side of heel and rem 8 heel sts. *76 sts.*
Work 1 round even.

DECREASE FOR INSTEP

K to last 4 sts on first needle, k2tog, k2; k across second needle; third needle: k2, k2tog tbl, k to end of needle.
Work 1 round even.
Cont in stripe patt, rep these 2 rounds until 14 sts remain on first and third needles. *54 sts.*
Slip last st of first needle onto beg of second needle. Work even until foot measures (from where sts were picked up at heel) 6 inches/15cm for a 9½–inch/24cm foot; 6½ inches/

16.5cm for a 10-inch/25cm foot; 7 inches/18cm for a 10½-inch/27cm foot.

SHAPE TOE

Round 1 K to last 3 sts of first needle, k2tog, k1; on second needle: k1, k2tog tbl, k to last 3 sts, k2tog, k1; on third needle: k1, k2tog tbl, k to end of needle.
Round 2 Work 1 round even.
Rep these two rounds until 26 sts rem in round.
K first 6 sts of round, then bind off sts from two needles together, or graft toe sts (see page 142).

Make another sock in the same way.

FINISHING

Block or press carefully (see page 143).

Turkish Socks

The patterns on these Turkish socks could be taken from the knotted carpets and woven kilims of the area, and they originated as early as the seventeenth century. Multicolored socks would have been worn by women; men wore plainer stockings with their knee breeches. Turkish socks have a construction of their own. The soles of these socks have a different pattern from the rest of the sock, which is knitted in the round from the toe upward, and has a triangular toe and a "peasant" heel worked in the opposite direction. We have made a version with only two colors in a round using a warm double-knitting wool; the stranded second color makes for a thick sock to be worn for lounging—when it is time to put your feet up.

❋ MATERIALS

Yarn

Rowan Pure Wool DK (100% super-wash
wool, 137 yards/125m):

2 [2, 2] 50g (1¾oz) balls, shade 010
Indigo (A)

1 [1, 2] 50g (1¾oz) ball, shade 008
Marine (B)

1 [1, 1] 50g (1¾oz) ball, shade 032 Gilt (C)

1 [1, 1] 50g (1¾oz) ball, shade 035
Quarry (D)

Needles

Set of four or five double-pointed needles
U.S. size 3/3.25mm

Set of five double-pointed needles U.S.
size 5/3.75mm

Set of four or five double-pointed needles
U.S. size 6/4mm

❋ MEASUREMENTS

To fit 9 [10, 10½]-inch/23 [25.5, 27.5]cm foot.
Length of leg from bottom of heel:
13 inches/33cm.

Gauge

26 sts and 28 rows measure 4 inches/10cm
over color pattern with yarn stranded
behind using size 5/3.75mm needles (or
size needed to obtain correct gauge).

❋ NOTE

These socks are knitted from the toe up.

Begin at the toe. Using medium-size
needles and C [D, D] cast on 8 sts
(4 sts onto each of two needles)
using the "figure-eight" cast-on
(see page 142).

Cont in C [D, D] working in rows
using three needles: two needles
carrying sts and the third needle
to knit with.

Row 1 (RS) K the 4 sts on the top
needle.

Row 2 (RS) Rotate needles and
k the 4 sts tbl on what was the
bottom needle.

Row 3 (RS) Rotate needles and
k the 4 sts worked in row 1.
There is now a piece of St st with
a needle at each end. This piece
continues to be worked sideways
as a side band along the foot while
the instep and sole are worked.
It is normal for the "figure-eight"

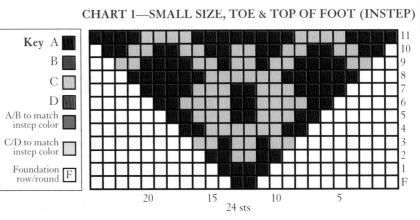

CHART 1—SMALL SIZE, TOE & TOP OF FOOT (INSTEP)

Key A
B
C
D
A/B to match instep color
C/D to match instep color
Foundation row/round [F]

24 sts

CHART 2—MEDIUM SIZE, TOE & TOP OF FOOT (INSTEP)

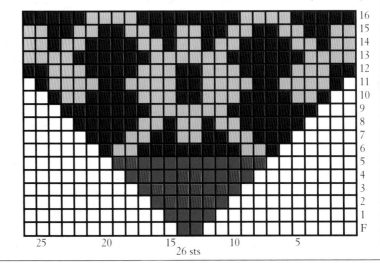

26 sts

CHART 3—LARGE SIZE, TOE & TOP OF FOOT (INSTEP)

22
21
20
19
18
17
16
15
14
13
12
11
10
9
8
7
6
5
4
3
2
1
F

28 sts   25   20   15   10   5

CHART 4—ALL SIZES, SOLES

23
22
21
20
19
18
17
16
15
14
13
12
11
10
9
8
7
6
5
4
3
2
1
F

29 sts   25   20   15   10   5

small size
medium size
large size

sts to be loose and enlarged. After a few rows, work the excess yarn toward the cast-on tail to achieve the correct gauge.

Join A [B, B] and work the foll foundation round (F) to begin to work in rounds on five needles: four needles carrying sts and the fifth needle to knit with.

Foundation round With RS of the St st piece facing, using A [B, B] and first empty needle, pick up and k 2 sts from the side edge of the 3 rows just worked to begin the instep (the F row of Chart 1 [2, 3]); using C [D, D] and second empty needle, k the 4 sts of the side band; using A [B, B] and third empty needle, pick up and k 3 sts from the second side edge to begin the sole (F row of chart 4); then using C [D, D] and fourth empty needle, k the 4 sts at the other end of the side band. *13 sts.*

Now work in rounds foll the charts as stated for each size.
Keep the instep, first side band, sole, and second side band sts each on a different needle.
The sole is worked using the same two colors as for the instep throughout.
The side bands are worked using C or D to match the instep and leg colors throughout the sock.

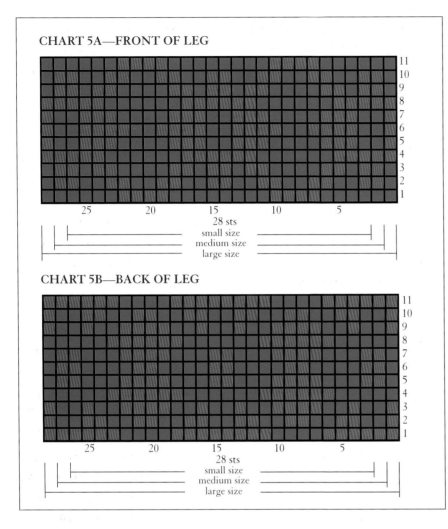

CHART 5A—FRONT OF LEG

28 sts

small size
medium size
large size

CHART 5B—BACK OF LEG

28 sts

small size
medium size
large size

To increase, pick up and k 1 st from the side edge of the 4-st side band. 4 sts for the side band are knitted in each row but only 2 sts will be visible on the sock after the pick up and k increase.

Round 1 Using A and C [B and D, B and D] work row 1 of Chart 1 [2, 3] for the instep as follows: using A [B, B] pick up and k 1 st from the side edge of the side band; using A [B, B] k2;

using A [B, B] pick up and k 1 st from the side edge of the side band; then using C [D, D] k 4 sts of first side band; then using A and C [B and D, B and D] work row 1 of Chart 4 for the sole as follows: using A [B, B] pick up and k 1 st from the side edge of the side band; using A [B, B] k1; using C [D, D] k1; using A [B, B] k1; using A [B, B] pick up and k 1 st from the side edge of the side band; then using C [D, D] k 4 sts of second side band. *17 sts.*

Rounds 2–11 [12, 13] Work as set foll the appropriate rows and colors of Charts 1 [2, 3] and 4. Toe shaping complete. *57 [61, 65] sts.*

SMALL SIZE

Round 12 (side band dec round) Using B and D work row 1 of Chart 5A for instep; using D work the 4 sts of the side band as (k2tog, ssk); using B and D work row 12 of Chart 4 for sole; then using D work the 4 sts of the side band as (k2tog, ssk). *53 sts.* Redistribute sts on the four working needles.

MEDIUM AND LARGE SIZES

Round [13, 14] (side band dec round) Using A and C work row [13, 14] of Chart [2, 3]; using C work the 4 sts of the side band as (k2tog, ssk); using A and C work row [13, 14] of Chart 4; then using C work the 4 sts of the side band as (k2tog, ssk). *[57, 61] sts.* Redistribute sts on the four working needles.

Round [14, 15] Using A and C work row [14, 15] of Chart [2, 3]; using C k2 sts of first side band; using A and C work row [14, 15] of Chart 4; then using C k 2 sts of second side band.

Rounds [15 and 16, 16–22] Using A and C work even as set foll the appropriate rows of Charts [2, 3] and 4.

Round [17, 23] Using B and D work row 1 of Chart 5A for instep; using D k 2 sts of first side band; using B and D work row [17, 23] of Chart 4 for sole; then using D k 2 sts of second side band.

ALL SIZES

Round 13 [18, 24] Using B and D work row 2 of Chart 5A for instep; using D k 2 sts of first side band; using B and D and keeping patt as set, work the 25 [27, 29] sts of sole; then using D k 2 sts of second side band. Maintaining continuity of patt throughout (instep, first side band, sole, second side band), and using the colors as shown in the charts, work even foll the instep patt sequence as follows:
Work rows 3–11 of Chart 5A.
Work rows 1–11 of Chart 6A.
Work rows 1–11 of Chart 5A.
Work rows 1–11 of Chart 6A.

SET POSITION FOR HEEL

Next round Using B and D work 24 [26, 28] sts of row 1 of Chart 5A for front of leg; then using D k 2 sts of first side band. Slip the 25 [27, 29] sts of the sole onto a stitch holder; then using B and D cast on 24 [26, 28] sts loosely using the thumb method (see page 139 and note below)

foll color pattern of row 1 of Chart 5B; then using D k 2 sts of second side band.

Note When casting on by the thumb method it is possible to reverse the tail and the main yarn colors as required to achieve the correct color sequence.

Next round Using B and D work 24 [26, 28] sts of row 2 of Chart 5A; using D k 2 sts of first side band; using B and D work 24 [26, 28] sts of row 2 of Chart 5B; then using B k 2 sts of second side band. Maintaining continuity of patt as set throughout (front of leg from Chart 5A, first side band, back of leg from Chart 5B, second side band), and using the colors as shown in the charts, work even foll the front of leg patt sequence as follows:
Work rows 3–11 of chart 5A.
Work rows 1–11 of chart 6A.
Work rows 1–11 of chart 5A.
Work rows 1–11 of chart 6A.

Next round Using B and D and medium-size needles work row 1 of Chart 5A; using D and medium-size needles k 2 sts of first side band; using B and D and largest needles work row 1 of Chart 5B; then using B and medium-size needles k 2 sts of second side band.

Using needle sizes as set and maintaining continuity of patt, work 5 more rounds foll rows 2–6 of Chart 5A or 5B as set.

Next round Using B and D and medium-size needles work row 7 of Chart 5A; using D and largest needles k 2 sts of first side band; using B and D and largest needles work row 7 of Chart 5B; then using B and largest needles k 2 sts of second side band. Using needle sizes as set and maintaining continuity of patt, work 4 more rounds foll rows 8–11 of Chart 5A or 5B as set.

Next round (row 1 of Chart 7) Using largest needles and A throughout, k 24 [26, 28] sts across front of leg; k 2 sts of first side band; M1 1 [0, 0] time, k2tog 0 [1, 0] time, k 24 [22, 28] sts across back of leg, M1 1 [0, 0] time, k2tog 0 [1, 0] time; then k 2 sts of second side band. *54 [54, 60] sts.* Using largest needles throughout and using A, C, and D as shown, work 16 rounds foll rows 2–17 of Chart 7, repeating the 6 sts 9 [9, 10] times. There are no side bands.

TOP RIBBING

Next round Using largest needles and B k all 54 [54, 60] sts.
Next round Using smallest needles and B *k1, p1; rep from * to end. Rep last round 8 more times to form

1x1 rib.

Bind off as follows: K1, p1, wyif slip both sts to left needle and p2tog, * k1, pass st already on right needle over st just worked, p1, wyif slip both sts to left needle and p2tog; rep from * to end. Fasten off. This gives an elastic edge.

HEEL

Slip the 25 [27, 29] sts of the sole held on a stitch holder onto the medium-size needles.

Round 1 Using medium-size needles and A, with RS of sole facing, pick up and k 1 st from side band, k1 from sole; using A and C and maintaining the continuity of the sole patt, work across 23 [25, 27] sts of the sole; using A k last st of sole; pick up and k 2 sts from side band; then pick up and k 1 st into the first cast-on st of the back of the leg; using A and C pick up and k 22 [24, 26] sts into the cast-on sts of the back of the leg foll row 1 of Chart 6B while at the same time matching the back of leg cast-on patt; using A pick up and k 1 st into the last cast-on st of the back of the leg, then using A pick up and k 1 st from side band. *53 [57, 61] sts.*

Round 2 Using A ssk, k1; using A and C patt 21 [23, 25] sts of sole; using A k1, k2tog, ssk, k1; using A and C patt

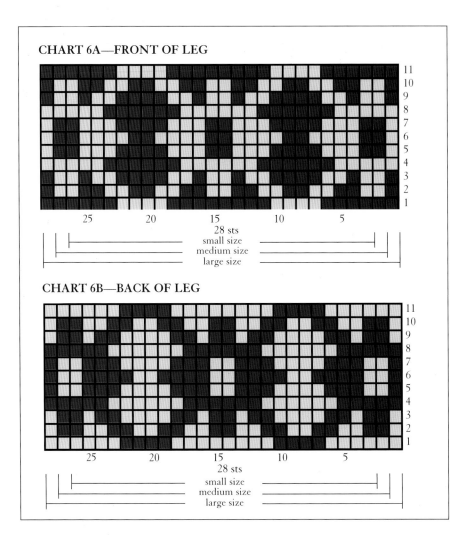

CHART 6A—FRONT OF LEG

CHART 6B—BACK OF LEG

20 [22, 24] sts of back of leg foll center 20 [22, 24] sts of row 2 of chart 6B; then using A k1, k2tog. *49 [53, 57] sts.* Working the k1 in A before and after the dec (also worked in A) minimizes the show-through of C at the sides of the heel.

Round 3 Using A ssk, k1; using A and C patt 19 [21, 23] sts of sole; using A k1, k2tog, ssk, k1; using A and C patt 18 [20, 22] sts of back of leg foll center 18 [20, 22] sts of row 3

of Chart 6B; then using A k1, k2tog. *45 [49, 53] sts.*

Maintaining continuity of patterning as set, including the k1 in A before and after the dec, cont to dec 4 sts in every round (when row 11 of Chart 6B has been worked, beg Chart 6B again from row 1), until the foll round has been worked:
Using A ssk, k1; using A and C patt 3 sts of sole; using A k1, k2tog, ssk,

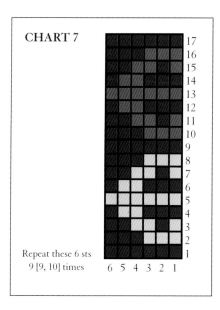

CHART 7

Repeat these 6 sts
9 [9, 10] times

k1; using A and C patt 2 sts of back of leg foll center 2 sts of appropriate row of Chart 6B; then using A k1, k2tog. *13 sts.*

Next round Using A ssk; using A and C patt 3 sts of sole; using A k2tog, ssk; using A and C patt 2 sts of back of leg foll center 2 sts of Chart 6B; then using A k2tog. *9 sts.* With decreases at the sides of the heel, using A graft the 4 sts at the back of the leg to the 5 sts on the sole (see page 142), working the center st on the sole with its adjacent sts to accommodate this extra st. Make another sock in the same way.

FINISHING

Sew in ends. With the side bands to the sides, block or press carefully (see page 143).

Striped & Fair Isle Socks

These socks, which feature stripes combined with small Fair Isle patterns, are knitted in a felted tweed yarn that has a soft handle and pretty, soft coloring, too; the Fair Isle patterns are the filler *peerie* patterns usually found between the larger motifs on sweaters and scarves. There is an element of viscose in the yarn, which will improve the wearing qualities, and the alpaca adds a luxury feel. Knitted in the round from the top down, the socks have a short-row heel; the stripes are narrow so that you do not have to break off your yarn, but you can avoid the "jog" at the end of the round by following the hint given in the pattern.

✳ MATERIALS

Yarn

Rowan Felted Tweed (50% merino wool, 25%
alpaca, 25% viscose, approx 191 yards/175m):
1 x 50g (approx 1¾oz) ball, shade 167 Maritime (A)
1 x 50g (approx 1¾oz) ball, shade 162 Clover (B)
1 x 50g (approx 1¾oz) ball, shade 164 Grey Mist (C)

Needles

Set of four double-pointed needles U.S. size
2/3mm
Set of four double-pointed needles U.S. size
3/3.5mm

✳ MEASUREMENTS

To fit 9-inch/23cm foot. For longer or
shorter sizes add or remove rounds
on foot (see pattern).
Length of leg from bottom of heel: 13 inches/33cm.

Gauge

26 sts and 32 rows measure 4 inches/10cm using
size 3/3.5mm needles (or size needed to obtain
correct gauge). Note: These socks were knitted
with metric needles; if you have trouble achieving
the correct gauge, try using metric needles.

✳ NOTE

Changing color while knitting in the round
creates a "jog," or visible join, at the beginning/
end of the round. To prevent this, first knit
one round of the new color; then, at the start of
the second round of the new color, slip the first
stitch purlwise and continue knitting.

Using larger needles and yarn A cast
on 60 sts, dividing them between
three needles. Join to work in the
round, being careful not to twist sts.
Use a stitch marker to mark the
start of the round, if you like.

Change to smaller needles and work
2 rounds in k2, p2 rib.
Change to B and cont in k2, p2 rib
for 3 rounds.
Change to A and cont in k2, p2 rib
for 3 rounds.

Change to larger needles and B and
k 3 rounds.
Change to A and k 3 rounds.
Repeat stripes in B and A until a
total of 5 stripes in St st have been
worked.

Work Chart 1 (15 rounds).

Starting with a stripe in B and
alternating with A, work 8 3-round
stripes in St st.
Work Chart 2 (15 rounds).
Starting and ending with a stripe
in A, work 5 more 3-round stripes,
alternating stripes in A and B.

HEEL

Change to smaller needles and B.
Knit 1 round.
Now work in rows.
Row 1 Sl 1 (to avoid jog), k13, wrap
and turn (see page 141). Slip next
30 sts onto a spare piece of yarn
for instep.
Row 2 Sl wrapped st, p28, wrap
and turn.
Row 3 Sl wrapped st, k27, wrap
and turn.
Rep rows 2 and 3 dec the number

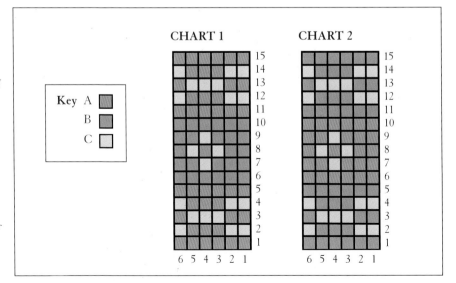

CHART 1   15 14 13 12 11 10 9 8 7 6 5 4 3 2 1
6 5 4 3 2 1

CHART 2   15 14 13 12 11 10 9 8 7 6 5 4 3 2 1
6 5 4 3 2 1

Key A
B
C

of sts worked on each row until you have 10 sts unwrapped in the middle and 10 sts wrapped at each end (row 20).

Working wraps together with sts, work as follows:

Row 21 Slip wrapped st, k11, wrap and turn.

Row 22 Slip wrapped st, p12, wrap and turn.

Rep rows 21 and 22 inc the number of sts worked on each row until all wrapped stitches have been worked (row 38).

FOOT

Change to larger needles.

Put 30 instep stitches on a needle and knit them. This becomes second needle. Working in the round, knit the rem 15 sts onto third needle. The stitch distribution on three needles is now 15, 30, 15, with the yarn at the center back between third needle and first needle.

Knit one more round in yarn B, then work one more stripe in A and one more stripe in B.

Work Chart 1, then work 4 more 3-round solid-colored stripes in A and B, starting with a stripe in B.

Note To make the socks fit a slightly larger or smaller foot, add or remove stripes at this point, working until foot measures approx 2½ inches/6cm less than the desired length.

SHAPE TOE

Change to B for next three rounds, then complete the toe in A.

Round 1 First needle: k to last 3 sts, k2tog, k1; second needle: k1, ssk, k to last 3 sts, k2tog, k1; third needle: k1, ssk, work to end.

Round 2 Knit.

Rep these two rounds until 32 sts rem (8, 16, 8).

Rep first round 3 more times; 20 sts rem (5, 10, 5).

K 5 sts on first needle.

Graft toe sts (see page 142) or bind off tog on the WS.

Make another sock in the same way.

FINISHING

Block or press carefully (see page 143).

Gansey Stitch Patterns

The patterns of the fisher ganseys and jerseys have been the subject of many publications, starting with Gladys Thompson's *Guernsey and Jersey Patterns*, published in 1955. In the 1980s there were also books on traditional knitwear by Richard Rutt, Rae Compton, and Michael Pearson, among others. The original guernsey sweaters, or ganseys, probably started life as plain jerseys, knitted in the Channel Islands for the Navy, but during the nineteenth century they were knitted by women in all the fishing ports of Britain. They were, by then, heavily patterned with their characteristic motifs reflecting the skill of the knitter and the lives of the fishermen.

The Scottish lassies would follow the fleet from port to port, from Scotland to Norfolk, and worked gutting the herrings. They knitted as they walked along the quay in the evenings, and patterns would be exchanged and copied, but there were always distinctive features to their jerseys. Some have all-over vertical patterns; others are patterned only on the yoke; the body is always knitted in the round, with the sleeves knitted down from the shoulder. The gusset in the underarm allows freedom of movement, and there is often a decorative "strap" where the shoulder is joined, sometimes with binding off visible on the outside. The sleeves, when worn out, could be unraveled and reknitted. There are seam stitches in purl worked in the sides, so that the pattern can be arranged identically back and front.

The patterns are always raised purl stitches on a stockinette-stitch background, unlike Aran, but there are often cables among the other patterns of Diamonds and Ladders, Fishing Nets, Starfish, Horseshoe, and Marriage Lines. Tree of Life and Anchor are other favorite designs, and some are named after the knitter who invented them.

The wool used was a 4- or 5-ply worsted, tightly spun, and tightly knitted so that it would "turn water." All the photographs of fishermen and lifeboat crews in the nineteenth century show men wearing these ganseys, and the women would knit both for their families and sometimes for sale. There were ganseys for work and ganseys for Sunday best. Fishermen were often Chapel-goers, because they could wear their ganseys there; in Cornwall, the Reverend Robert Hawker wore his gansey under his coat to show that he was a "fisher of men."

Perhaps the most highly patterned ganseys come from Eriskay, a tiny island in the Outer Hebrides of Scotland. These use vertical patterns in the body, and the yoke is divided into squares above a chest band of net patterns. The necks are buttoned, a distinguishing feature. The Scottish Merchant used to sell the output of a group of knitters on the island, but 20 years later there is just one knitter making the Eriskay ganseys, and she has made the lovely stockings on page 68. It is tragic to think that in the future these jerseys will cease to be made.

Gansey Stitch Socks with Gusset Heel

These textured socks, which reflect the stitches used on fishermen's ganseys, are knitted with a wool and cotton blend that gives good definition to the stitch pattern. There are purl seam stitches down the back to help you keep the pattern correct, and the patterns down the front—of Diamonds and the Cross or Starfish—are a feature of the jerseys made in the Western Isles of Scotland. There is a different pattern of textured stitches in the welt, similar to guernsey welts; even the shade of yarn we have chosen is reminiscent of the lovely rust-colored canvas sails of the old fishing boats that worked around the little ports of Scotland and the north of England.

✳ MATERIALS

Yarn

*Rowan Wool Cotton (50% merino wool,
50% cotton, approx 123 yards/113m):
4 x 50g (1¾ oz) balls, shade 966
Chestnut*

Needles

*Set of four double-pointed needles U.S.
size 5/3.75mm*

✳ MEASUREMENTS

*To fit 9½-inch/24cm foot (adjustable).
Length of leg from bottom of heel:
13½ inches/34cm.*

Gauge

*22 sts and 32 rows
measure 4 inches/10cm
using size 5/3.75mm
needles (or size needed
to obtain correct gauge).*

Cast on
52 sts and
join, being careful
not to twist sts.
Round 1 Purl.
Round 2 Knit.
Rep these 2 rounds twice more,
then work in rib as follows:
P1, (k2, p2) to last 3 sts, k2, p1.
Cont as set for 7 more rounds.
Keeping the first and last sts in purl
to form seam stitches down the
back, work 7 rounds knit.
Work 1 round purl, dec 1 st in this
round. *51 sts.*

Now foll patt as on chart.

HEEL

At round 59 of chart inc in each of
the seam sts to start a gusset for the
heel, while maintaining the chart
patt down the center panel. *53 sts.*

Work the inc sts as knit from now
on, so round 60 will start k1, p1,
then cont to follow the patt as set,
to last 2 sts, p1, k1.
Inc on every 3rd round, picking up
and knitting into the right loop of
the k st of the round below, then
cont in patt as set to last 2 sts, p1,
k into front and back of next st,
until there is a total of 22 sts in the
gusset. *75 sts.*
Rearrange the sts so that all the
gusset k sts are on one needle.

Turn heel:
With RS facing, turn heel using
short-row shaping (see page 141)
as follows:
Row 1 K14, wrap next st and turn.
Row 2 Sl 1 p-wise, p6, wrap next st,
turn.
Row 3 Sl 1 p-wise, k7, wrap next st,
turn.
Row 4 Sl 1 p-wise, p8, wrap next
stitch, turn.
Cont to dec in this way on every row
until all the gusset sts are used.
Cont working in rounds, keeping
central 27 sts in patt as on chart and

the rest in St st, and dec 1 st at each side of central 27 on every other row until a total of 53 sts remain.

TOE

When foot measures 8 inches/20cm from back of heel or 1½ inches/4cm less than desired length, dec for toe as follows:

Rearrange the sts so that you have the 26 k sts for the sole divided equally between two adjacent needles. Start the round working from the center of the sole. K11, k2tog, work central 27 stitches from chart, ssk, knit to end. Work a dec before and after the central patt on the foll 6 rounds as follows:

Next round K5, k2tog, patt 6, ssk, patt 11, k2tog, patt 6, ssk, k to end. Cont to dec in this way to 21 sts.

Divide work between two needles and dec 1 st at center of second needle. *20 sts.*
Graft toe sts (see page 142) or bind off tog on the WS.

Make another sock in the same way.

FINISHING

Block or press carefully (see page 143).

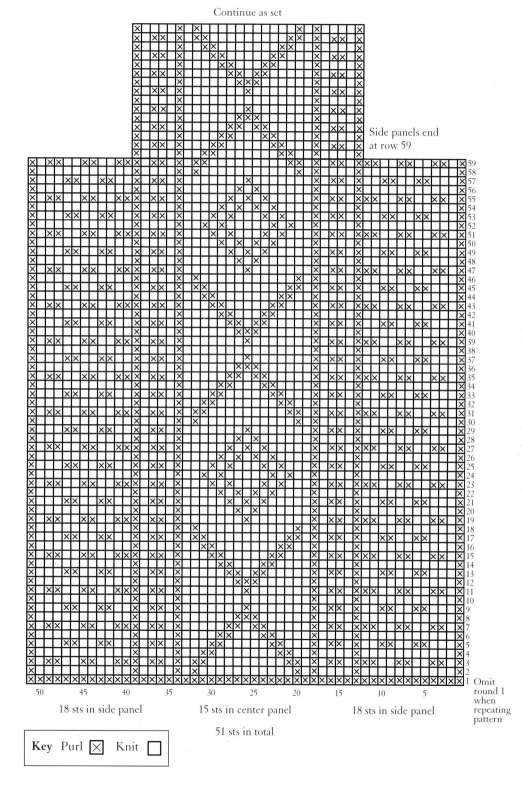

Continue as set

Side panels end at row 59

Omit round 1 when repeating pattern

50 45 40 35 30 25 20 15 10 5

18 sts in side panel

15 sts in center panel

18 sts in side panel

51 sts in total

Key Purl ⊠ Knit ☐

Gansey Stitch Socks with Buttons

These socks were designed for us by Rita Taylor, who became interested in gansey patterns when she lived in the north-east of England—originally home to many of the fishing villages that had their own traditional gansey stitch patterns. She has chosen a Ladder and Diamond pattern in seed stitch, which was popular in Yorkshire, and combined it with a buttoned rib, which is traditionally used on the necks of Scottish jerseys. The authentic 5-ply gansey wool makes for a cozy and sturdy sock for boots, beaches, and boating. The lovely denim blue is that appealing faded shade, and the wool is from British breeds of sheep, spun in Yorkshire.

✳ MATERIALS

Yarn

British Breeds Traditional Guernsey 5-ply (100% pure new British wool, worsted spun, approx 242 yards/224m): 2 x 100g (3½ oz) balls, shade G503 Denim

Needles

*One pair U.S. size 2/3mm needles
Set of four double-pointed needles
U.S. size 3/3mm*

Notions

4 buttons, ½ inch/1.25cm in diameter

✳ MEASUREMENTS

*To fit 8½ [9½, 10]-inch/22 [24, 25]cm foot.
Length of leg from bottom of heel:
14½ inches/37cm.*

Gauge

26 sts and 36 rows measure 4 inches/10cm using size 3/3mm needles (or size needed to obtain correct gauge). Note: These socks were knitted with metric needles; if you have trouble achieving the correct gauge, try using metric needles.

RIGHT SOCK

Using two needles, cast on 72 sts and work 3 rows in k2, p2 rib.
Buttonhole row 1 K2, bind off 2, rib to end.
Buttonhole row 2 Rib to last 4 sts, cast on 2, p2.
Work 4 rows rib, then rep 2 buttonhole rows again.
** Work 2 more rows in rib.
Next row Slip all sts, apart from last 6, onto three double-pointed needles. Overlap the first 6 sts with these last 6 sts and k them together. K to end of round. *66 sts.*
Rearrange sts so that last 12 and first 10 are on first needle; next 22 are on second needle; and next 22 are on third needle. Place a marker between first and third needles to show beg of round.
Knit 8 rounds even.
Now foll chart:
Continue for 60 rounds (a total of 5 pattern repeats).
Knit 2 rounds even.

DECREASE FOR ANKLE

Round 1 P1, k1, k2tog, k to last 4 sts, k2tog tbl, k1, p1.
Rounds 2 and 3 P1, k to last st, p1.

Rep these 3 rounds until 56 sts remain, then rep round 2 until leg measures 11 inches/28cm (or desired length).

HEEL

K14, turn, sl 1, p27.
Cont in St st on these 28 sts, always slipping first st, for a total of 24 rows.

Turn heel:
Next row Sl 1, p14, p2tog, p1.
Next row Sl 1, k3, k2tog tbl, k1.
Next row Sl 1, p4, p2tog, p1.
Next row Sl 1, k5, k2tog tbl, k1.

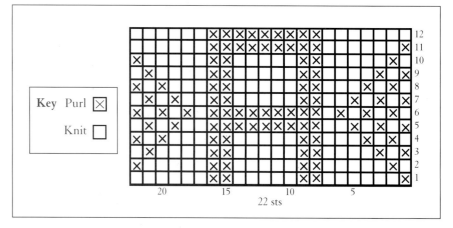

Cont in this way, working 1 more st before the dec until the row "Sl 1, k13, k2tog tbl, k1" has been worked. *16 sts.*

INSTEP

Place all instep sts on one needle. With same needle, pick up and k 13 sts from along side of heel. With second needle, k 28 sts from instep; with third needle, pick up and k 13 sts along other side of heel, then k 8 sts from first needle. Knit 1 round even.

Next round first needle: k to last 3 sts, k2tog, k1; second needle: k to end; third needle, k1, k2tog tbl, k to end.

Rep these 2 rounds until 56 sts remain, then cont without dec until sock measures 6 [6¾, 8] inches/ 15 [17, 20]cm from back of heel.

SHAPE TOE

Dec round 1 *K5, k2tog; rep from * to end.
Knit 5 rounds even.
Dec round 2 *K4, k2tog; rep from * to end.
Knit 4 rounds even.
Dec round 3 *K3, k2tog; rep from * to end.
Knit 3 rounds even.

Dec round 4 *K2, k2tog; rep from * to end.
Knit 2 rounds even.
Last dec round *K1, k2tog; rep from * to end.
Knit 1 round.
Knit 4 sts from first needle onto third needle so that there are 8 sts on each needle. Graft (see page 142) or bind off sts tog on the WS.

LEFT SOCK

Work as for right sock but make buttonholes at the end of the 4th row as follows:

Buttonhole row 1 Rib to last 4 sts, bind off 2, k2.
Buttonhole row 2 P2, cast on 2, rib to end.
Work 4 rows then rep 2 buttonhole rows again.
Complete as for right sock from ** to end.

FINISHING

Sew on buttons to correspond with buttonholes.
Block or press carefully (see page 143).

Eriskay Stockings

The island of Eriskay is home to the most ornate of all the fishermen's ganseys, and these socks were knitted for us there in the traditional 5-ply guernsey wool. Eriskay is a tiny island between the Outer Hebridean islands of Barra and South Uist, and in the past it relied entirely on fishing; the patterns on the ganseys from Eriskay often feature motifs that reflect the lives of the fishermen. Here, however, we have Marriage Lines and Diamonds, which are also traditional to ganseys of this area. The cream wool shows up the patterns, and is a hardwearing worsted-spun yarn, just right for country walks as well as seafaring.

✳ MATERIALS

Yarn

Wendy (Poppleton's) 5-ply Guernsey wool (100% worsted wool, approx 245 yards/224m): 2 x 100g (3½oz) balls, shade Cream

Needles

Set of four double-pointed needles U.S. size 2/2.75mm

Special Abbreviation

pyo1 or pyo2 Pass yarn over 1 st or pass yarn over 2 sts. Worked in this sequence: yo, k1, pyo1; the yarn that you bring over the needle creates a strand before the knit st; this strand is lifted and passed over the knit st after it has been worked. The instruction "pyo2" is worked in the same way, except that the strand is lifted over the 2 following knit sts.

✳ MEASUREMENTS

To fit 9-inch/23cm foot (adjustable). Length of leg from bottom of heel: 12½ inches/32cm.

Gauge

26 stitches and 36 rows measure 4 inches/ 10cm using size 2/2.75mm needles (or size needed to obtain correct gauge).

Cast on 62 sts, divide between three needles, and join, being careful not to twist sts. Work 2 inches/5cm in k1, p1 rib, knitting the knit sts through the back loop. Knit 1 round. Put 31 sts on one needle for patt at front and divide the rest between two needles for plain back. Work the 31 patt sts for front as follows, working the remaining 31 sts plain knit.

The pattern across the front is made up as follows (see chart):

8 sts for Marriage Lines (first repeat), pattern A
3 sts Seed Stitch, pattern B
9 sts for Diamond Patterns, pattern C
3 sts Seed Stitch, pattern B
8 sts Marriage Lines (second repeat), pattern A (total 31 sts).

PATTERN A: MARRIAGE LINES, **FIRST REPEAT**

Round 1 P1, k1, p1, k5.
Round 2 P1, k1, p2, k4.
Round 3 P1, k2, p2, k3.

Round 4 P1, k3, p2, k2.

Round 5 P1, k4, p2, k1.

Round 6 P1, k5, p1, k1.

Round 7 P1, k7.

PATTERN A: MARRIAGE LINES, SECOND REPEAT

Round 1 K1, p1, k5, p1.

Round 2 K1, p2, k4, p1.

Round 3 K2, p2, k3, p1.

Round 4 K3, p2, k2, p1.

Round 5 K4, p2, k1, p1.

Round 6 K5, p1, k1, p1.

Round 7 K7, p1.

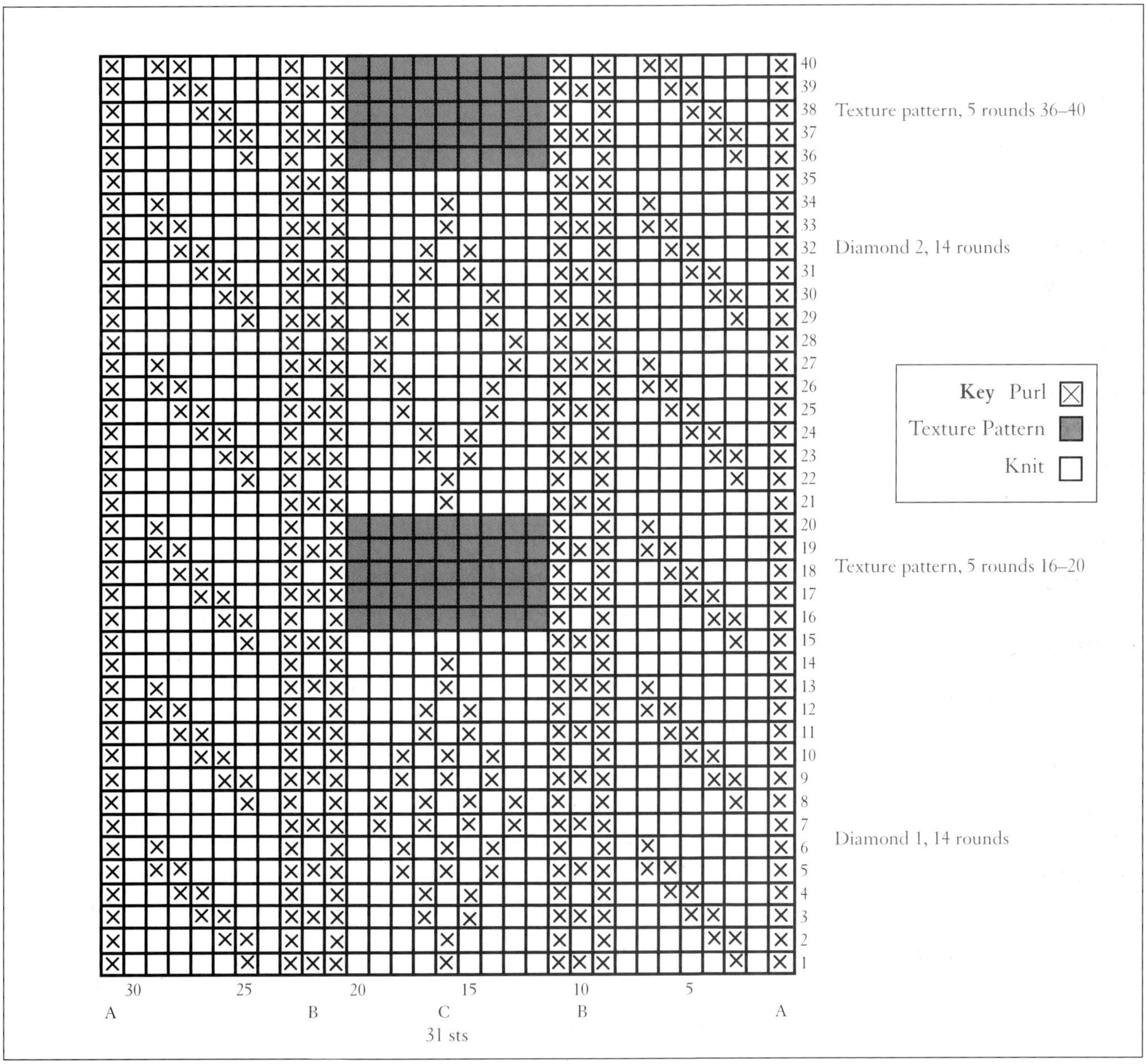

Texture pattern, 5 rounds 36–40

Diamond 2, 14 rounds

Key Purl ☒

Texture Pattern ▨

Knit ☐

Texture pattern, 5 rounds 16–20

Diamond 1, 14 rounds

31 sts

PATTERN B: SEED STITCH

Round 1 P3.

Round 2 P1, k1, p1.

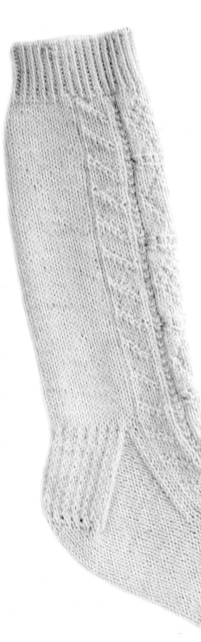

PATTERN C: CENTRAL DIAMOND PATTERNS

Rounds 1 and 2 K4, p1, k4.

Rounds 3 and 4 K3, p1, k1, p1, k3.

Rounds 5 and 6 K2, p1, k1, p1, k1, p1, k2.

Rounds 7 and 8 K1, p1, k1, p1, k1, p1, k1, p1, k1.

Rounds 9 and 10 K2, p1, k1, p1, k1, p1, p2.

Rounds 11 and 12 K3, p1, k1, p1, k3.

Rounds 13 and 14 K4, p1, k4.

Round 15 Knit.

Round 16 (Yo, k2, pyo2) twice, yo, k1, pyo1.

Round 17 (Yo, k2, pyo2) twice.

Round 18 Knit.

Round 19 As round 16.

Round 20 As round 17.

Rounds 21 and 22 K4, p1, k4.

Rounds 23 and 24 K3, p1, k1, p1, k3.

Rounds 25 and 26 K2, p1, k3, p1, k2.

Rounds 27 and 28 K1, p1, k5, p1, k1.

Rounds 29 and 30 As round 25.

Rounds 31 and 32 As round 23.

Rounds 33 and 34 As round 21.

Round 35 Knit.

Rounds 36–40 As rounds 16–20.

Keeping the panels in position as set (A, B, C, B, A), work in patt foll chart or written instructions until leg measures 10 1/4 inches/26cm. Divide the central 31 patt sts over two needles and leave for instep. Place rem 31 sts on one needle for heel.

HEEL

Next row Dec 1 st then work sl 1, k1 to end.

Next row Purl.

Rep these 2 rows for 2 inches/5cm. Turn heel:

Row 1 K12, k2tog, k2, skp, k12.

Row 2 Purl.

Row 3 K10, k2tog, k4, skp, k10.

Row 4 Purl.

Row 5 K8, k2tog, k6, skp, k8.

Row 6 Purl.

Cont in this way dec on every alt row until you have worked "K2tog, k14, skp."

Purl 1 row then knit across 16 sts with same needle.

Pick up and k 18 sts down left side of heel. Work in patt as set across 31 sts. With spare needle pick up and k 18 sts up right side of heel, knit 8. *83 sts.*

Next round K23, k2tog, k1, patt 31, k1, skp, k23.

Next round First needle: knit; second needle: pattern; third needle: knit.

Cont in this way dec 1 st at end of first needle and beg of third needle until 63 sts remain.

Next round Dec 1 st at end of first needle only. *62 sts*.

Complete the rest of the sock in stockinette st only.

SHAPE TOE

Next round First needle: k to last 3 sts, k2tog, k1; second needle: k1, skp, k to last 3 sts, k2tog, k1; third needle: k1, skp, k to end.

Next round Knit.

Cont to dec as above on every second round until you have 26 sts. Then dec on every round until you have 14 sts. Divide these sts between two needles, and graft (see page 143) or bind off sts tog.

Note This knitter has made her bind-off on the outside of the toe, which is traditional for this pattern.

FINISHING

Block or press carefully (see page 143).

Fair Isle & Sanquhar

The Shetland sheep come in a number of colors, ranging from dark brown, called natural black, through grays and fawns to the mid-brown called *moorit*. Some of these have lovely Shetland names such as *shaela* and *sholmit* (dark and light gray) and *eesit* and *mooskit* (shades of fawn). The early Shetland knitters also dyed their wool, the most common colors being a rich rust-red from madder and an indigo blue. Yellow from onion or lichen was also much used.

Many legends have grown up about the origin of the patterns, but as the Shetland Islands lie at the crossroads of a number of early shipping routes, these would have brought sailors from Scandinavia and the Baltic countries, among other places, including Eastern Europe, where patterned knitting was well established. By the early nineteenth century travelers to Shetland remarked on the brightly colored and patterned caps worn by the fishermen, and Sir Walter Scott wrote about the Fair Isle women who knitted stockings and caps.

The all-over patterned Fair Isle jersey suddenly became fashionable in 1922, when the Prince of Wales wore one playing golf at St. Andrews, and also sat for a portrait by John Lander wearing a Fair Isle sweater. This was a boon for the Shetland knitters, as the fashion must have given employment to a large number of women who were supplying the clothing shops in Lerwick, from where the knits were exported to the south.

Fair Isle patterns are distinctive in having only two colors in a round, the second color always being stranded at the back. The large hexagonal shapes and crosses make up the OXO design found in many of the old jerseys, divided by rows of small (or *peerie*) patterns. Knitting in the round has the advantage of the design always facing the knitter, and makes the garment seamless. The sleeves of jerseys are picked up from the shoulders in a similar way to the gansey fishermen's sweaters.

By the 1960s the old, strong Fair Isle patterns were being lost and Scandinavian patterns became popular. Fortunately, The Scottish Merchant made contact with Margaret Stuart, who had established a group of knitters and who supplied us with knitwear using traditional patterns and colors, often based on garments from the nineteenth century.

There are gloves in the Shetland Museum that resemble the Sanquhar patterns of Dumfriesshire, Scotland, showing how patterns travel. These are usually knitted in two colors, a dark and a contrast lighter shade, and are checked or plaid patterns with solid-colored borders. In Victorian days cottage industries flourished there, and Sanquhar was famous for its gloves and stockings. The five sock patterns in this chapter preserve an old craft—a hand-knitting tradition in danger of being lost.

Natural Fair Isle Socks

These beautiful socks display the natural colors of the Shetland sheep, and, unusually, the pattern runs vertically. This pattern, dating from about 1890, features in *The Complete Book of Traditional Fair Isle Knitting* by Sheila McGregor, where it is described as photographed at Sand Lodge, Sandwick. Since then it has been known as the Sand Lodge pattern, and Margaret Stuart has had it knitted again for this book. There is more work in these vertical patterns, as there are no plain-colored rounds, and this is particularly challenging because the zigzag pattern and the large OXO pattern have a different number of rounds in their pattern repeat.

✴ MATERIALS

Yarn

Jamieson's Shetland Spindrift (sweater weight), Natural Collection (100% Shetland wool, approx 115 yards/105m):

2 x 25g (approx 1oz) balls, shade 104 Natural White (A)

2 x 25g (approx 1oz) balls, shade 108 Moorit (B)

2 x 25g (approx 1oz) balls, shade 105 Eesit (C)

2 x 25g (approx 1oz) balls, shade 101 Shetland Black (D)

Needles

Set of four double-pointed needles U.S. size 2/3mm

✴ MEASUREMENTS

To fit 10-inch/25cm foot. Note: To reduce length of foot by approx ½inch/1.3cm omit the last 5 rounds of pattern 2. To reduce by approx 1 inch/2.5cm omit the last whole pattern. Length of leg from bottom of heel: 14½ inches/37cm.

Gauge

32 sts and 33 rows measure 4 inches/10cm over pattern using size 2/3mm needles (or size needed to obtain correct gauge). Note: These socks were knitted with metric needles; if you have trouble achieving the correct gauge, try using metric needles.

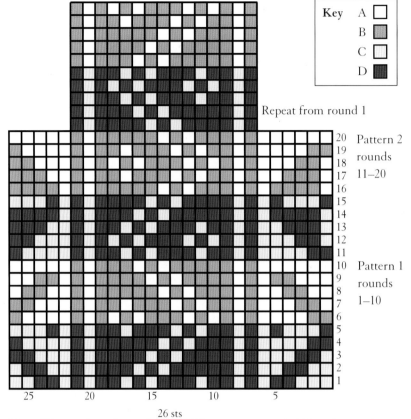

Continue with the zigzag pattern as before, repeating from round 7 or 19 but keeping the 5-row repeat of the background color to match the side patterns.

Key A
     B
     C
     D

Repeat from round 1

20
19
18   Pattern 2
17   rounds
16   11–20
15
14
13
12
11
10
9   Pattern 1
8   rounds
7   1–10
6
5
4
3
2
1

25   20   15   10   5

26 sts

Note: The number of rows in the OXO pattern repeat is 10 but the number of rows in the zigzag pattern is 12, so this will move up the 5-row background color as the pattern progresses.

Using A, cast on 64 sts and divide them between three needles; join, being careful not to twist sts. Place a marker at beg of round. Working in k2, p1 rib, knit 24 rounds as follows:
4 rounds in A, 6 rounds in B, 4 rounds in C, 6 rounds in D, 4 rounds in A.

Change to yarn C and knit 1 round inc as follows:
(Inc 1 in next st, k4, inc 1 in next st, k3) 6 times; inc 1 in next st, k4, inc 1 in next st, k4. *78 sts.*
Follow the chart for the Fair Isle leg pattern for 70 rounds. There are 3 repeats of the chart pattern around the sock.

HEEL

Divide the sts in two. Put center group of 39 sts on a spare needle or thread to hold. Work the heel on remaining 39 sts.

Work heel in C and D alternately: 1 st C, 1 st D as follows:

Work 18 rows St st.

Next row K27, k2tog, turn.

Next row P16, p2tog, turn.

Next row K16, k2tog, turn.

Cont in this way until all sts are worked onto one needle again.

Last row K2tog, k to last 2 sts, k2tog. *15 sts*.

Break off yarn.

Rejoin yarn at top right-hand side of heel flap. With RS of work facing, pick up and k 12 sts along edge of heel, k across center 15 sts, pick up and k 12 sts on other side of heel flap, k across 39 sts held on spare needle or thread. *78 sts*.

Rearrange sts over three needles with marker at center back.

Knit 1 round.

FOOT

Work foll the chart, starting with Pattern 2, and work 5 pattern repeats (50 rounds). For a smaller foot omit half or all of last pattern before toe.

TOE

Round 1 Using C k to end.

Round 2 Using D (k2tog, k4, k2tog, k3) 6 times, (k2tog, k4) twice. *64 sts*.

Next round Work in C and D alternately: 1 st C, 1 st, rep to end.

Next round Cont to work in alt colors as before: (k12, k2tog, k4, k2tog, k12) twice.

Cont to dec by working one less st each time, e.g. k11, k2tog, k4, k2tog, k11 until "k2tog, k4, k2tog" has been worked and 12 sts remain.

Divide sts onto two needles and graft (see page 142) or bind off sts tog on the WS across toe.

Make another sock in the same way.

FINISHING

Block or press carefully (see page 143). Because the sock is knitted straight, it is advisable to shape it while damp on a sock blocker to make the calf wider and the ankle narrower.

OXO Pattern Fair Isle Socks

These brightly colored socks have the large horizontal patterns often used in Fair Isle knitting, and feature the traditional madder red and indigo blue colors. The patterns are different all the way down the leg and the foot, and skilled knitters prided themselves on not repeating a pattern in their work. The large patterns—all variations on the OXO motif—are separated by two small *peerie* patterns, as is usual, and the toe and heel continue in one stitch dark, one stitch light, which the Shetland knitters call "loop by loop." A pair of Fair Isle socks very like this is in the textile collection at London's Victoria and Albert Museum; Margaret Stuart has re-created this beautiful pattern for us.

* MATERIALS

Yarn

Jamieson and Smith's Jumper [sweater] Weight (100% Shetland wool, approx 125 yards/115m):

1 x 25g (approx 1oz) ball, shade 5 Shetland Black (A)

Jamieson's Shetland Spindrift (sweater weight) (100% Shetland wool, approx 115 yards/105m):

1 x 25g (approx 1oz) ball, shade 289 Gold (B)

2 x 25g (approx 1oz) balls, shade 587 Madder (C)

1 x 25g (approx 1oz) ball, shade 726 Prussian Blue (D)

2 x 25g (approx 1oz) balls, shade 104 Natural White (E)

Needles

Set of four double-pointed needles U.S. size 3/3mm

* MEASUREMENTS

To fit 10-inch/25cm foot. Note: To reduce length of foot by ½ inch/1.25cm omit rounds 44–50 on the foot chart.

Length of leg from bottom of heel: 17½ inches/44.5cm. Note: For longer leg add another 7 rows by inserting the small pattern 1 after the ribbing.

Gauge

32 sts and 33 rows measure 4 inches/10cm over pattern using size 3/3mm needles (or size needed to obtain correct gauge). Note: These socks were knitted with metric needles.

Using E cast on 64 sts and divide them between three needles; join, being careful not to twist sts. Place a marker at the beg of the round. Working in k2, p2 rib, knit 30 rounds as follows:

4 rounds in E, 6 rounds in C,

4 rounds E, 6 rounds in D,

4 rounds in E, 6 rounds in C.

Knit 1 round in C, inc in every 4th st until there are 80 sts (16 incs).

Follow the chart for the Fair Isle leg patterns for 91 rounds.

Note Some of the larger Fair Isle patterns do not fit evenly into the total number of sts; just end the patt and start the beg of each round at the beg of the chart.

On the last patterned round before the heel, dec 4 sts as follows: (K2tog, k18) 4 times. *76 sts.*

HEEL

Divide the sts in two. Put center group of 38 sts on a spare needle or thread to hold. Work heel on the other 38 sts. Working in A and E alternately: 1 st A, 1 st E throughout heel, work 18 rows St st.

Next row K25, k2tog, turn.

Next row P14, p2tog, turn.

Next row K14, k2tog, turn.

Cont in this way until all sts are worked onto one needle again.

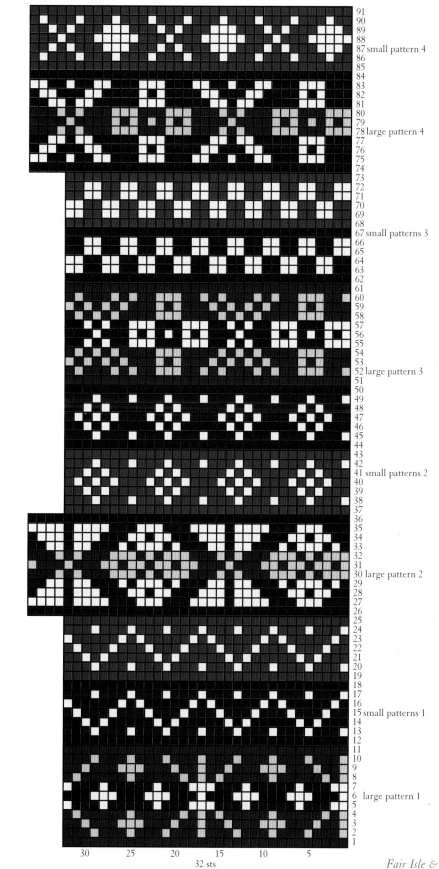

91
90
89
88
87 small pattern 4
86
85
84
83
82
81
80
79
78 large pattern 4
77
76
75
74
73
72
71
70
69
68
67 small patterns 3
66
65
64
63
62
61
60
59
58
57
56
55
54
53
52 large pattern 3
51
50
49
48
47
46
45
44
43
42
41 small patterns 2
40
39
38
37
36
35
34
33
32
31
30 large pattern 2
29
28
27
26
25
24
23
22
21
20
19
18
17
16
15 small patterns 1
14
13
12
11
10
9
8
7
6 large pattern 1
5
4
3
2
1

Key

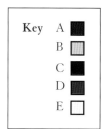

A
B
C
D
E

30   25   20   15   10   5

32 sts

Last row P to last 2 sts, p2tog. *14 sts.* Break off yarn.

Rejoin yarn to top of right-hand side of heel flap. With RS of work facing, pick up and k 12 sts along edge of heel, k across 14 heel sts, pick up and k 12 sts on other side of heel flap, k across 38 sts held on spare needle or thread. *76 sts.* Rearrange sts over three needles with marker at center back. Knit 1 round.

FOOT

Work foll the chart for the foot patterns for 50 rounds. For a shorter foot omit last small pattern before toe (i.e. 7 rounds), making 43 rounds.

TOE

Round 1 Using A knit to end.
Round 2 Using A (k4, k2tog) 12 times, to last 4 sts, k4. *64 sts.*
Next round Knit using A and E alternately: k1 A, k1 E, rep to end.
Next round Cont to work in alt colors for each st as previously (k12, k2tog, k4, k2tog, k12) twice. Cont by working 1 st less each time, e. g. k11, k2tog, k4, k2tog, k11 until "k2tog, k4, k2tog" has been worked and 12 sts remain. Divide sts onto two needles and graft (see page 142) or bind off sts tog on the WS across toe.

Make another sock in the same way.

FINISHING

Block or press carefully (see page 143). Because the sock is knitted straight, it is advisable to shape it while damp on a sock blocker to make the calf wider and the ankle narrower.

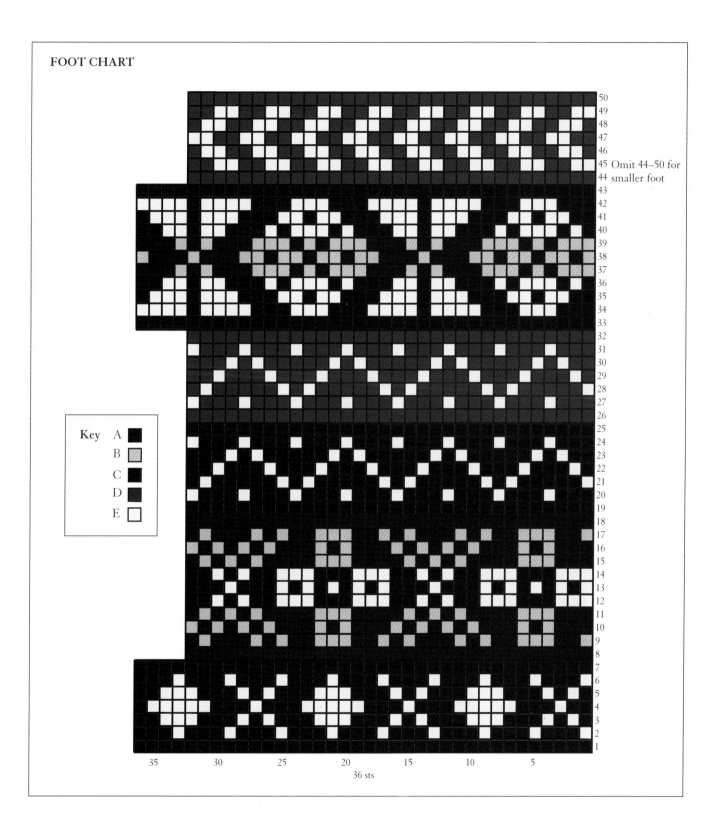

Omit 44–50 for smaller foot

Key
A
B
C
D
E

36 sts

Sanquhar Pattern Socks

The Royal Burgh of Sanquhar is a small town in Dumfriesshire, Scotland, which was noted for worsted stockings and gloves in the eighteenth and nineteenth centuries. There were many patterns, originally knitted in the natural black and white, and this one is known as Shepherd's Plaid. The cuffs of stockings or gloves were always patterned in stripes or contrasting checks, and often had the initials of the wearer worked into them. We have chosen a soft wool and cotton yarn in a pretty berry color contrasting with off-white, to give a fresh look to this traditional pattern.

✳ MATERIALS

Yarn

Rowan Wool Cotton (50% merino wool, 50% cotton, 123 yards/113m):

2 x 50g (1¾oz) balls, shade 969 Bilberry (A)

2 x 50g (1¾oz) balls, shade 900 Antique (B)

Needles

Set of four double-pointed needles U.S. size 2/2.75mm

Set of four double-pointed needles U.S. size 3/3.25mm

✳ MEASUREMENTS

To fit 9½–10-inch/24–25cm foot.

Length of leg from bottom of heel: 13 inches/33cm.

Gauge

28 sts and 28 rows measure 4 inches/10cm over main pattern using size 3/3.25mm needles (or size needed to obtain correct gauge).

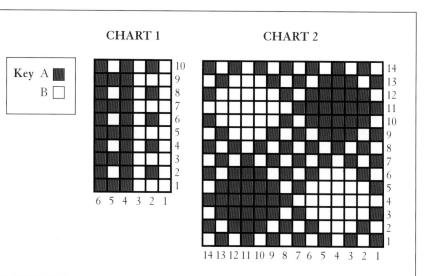

Using smaller needles and yarn A, cast on 72 sts. Arrange these sts on three needles and join, being careful not to twist sts.

CHART 1, BORDER PATTERN

Rounds 1–10 Working with A and B, follow rows 1–10

Round 11 Rep row 1.

Round 12 Rep row 2, dec 1 st at beg and end of round. *70 sts.*

Change to larger needles.

CHART 2, MAIN PATTERN

Next rounds Follow rows 1–7.

***Next rounds** Follow row 8, dec 1 st at beg and end of round.

Next rounds Follow rows 9–14.

Next round Rep row 1, dec 1 st at beg and end of round.

Next rounds Work 6 more rounds, foll rows 2–7.*

Rep from * to * until 56 sts remain, keeping patt correct.

Work 7 more rounds of Chart 2, inc 1 st at end of last round. *57 sts.*

Divide for heel:

K13, slip last 14 sts of round onto other end of same needle. *27 sts.*

Divide rem sts onto two needles and leave for instep. *30 sts.*

HEEL

Working on 27 sts, and keeping patt correct, work as follows:

Row 1 Follow row 8 of Chart 2.

Row 2 Follow row 7 of Chart 2.

Rep these two rows 10 more times and then rep row 1.

Turn heel:

Using patt established above, work as follows:

Row 1 K19, skp, turn.

Row 2 P12, P2tog, turn.

Row 3 K12, skp, turn.

Row 4 P12, P2tog, turn.

Cont in this way until all sts are worked onto one needle again. *13 sts.* Knit 1 row.

Slip all instep sts onto one needle. Using an empty needle, slip last 6 sts from heel onto this needle. Then pick up and k 16 sts along side of heel, working 1 st in A and 1 st in B alternately.

Using second needle, k across 30 instep sts, foll Chart 2.

Using third needle, pick up and k 16 sts along second side of heel, working 1 st in A and 1 st in B alternately, then k rem 7 sts from heel. *75 sts.*

SHAPE INSTEP

Using patt established for heel on first and third needles, and Chart 2 on second needle, cont as follows:

Round 1 Knit.

Round 2 First needle: k to last 3 sts, k2tog, k1; second needle, k foll Chart 2; third needle: k1, skp, k to end. Rep these two rounds until 59 sts remain.

Work even until work measures 6½ inches/16.5cm from where sts were picked up at heel.

SHAPE TOE

Round 1 First needle: k to last 3 sts, k2tog, k1; second needle: keeping patt correct, k1, skp, k to last 3 sts, k2tog, k1; third needle: k1, skp, k to end.

Round 2 Knit.

Rep these 2 rounds until 31 sts remain, then work one more row dec 1 st at beg of second needle. Divide 30 sts evenly between two needles. Graft (see page 142) or bind off tog both sets of sts.

Make another sock in the same way.

FINISHING

Block or press carefully (see page 143).

Cross & Flower Fair Isle Socks

This pattern was used in my previous book, *Country Weekend Knits*, to make a warm sweater in the same double-knitting wool, which gives the Fair Isle patterns a bolder look. The woodland shades are a new take on the old colors, but the striped ribs and OXO patterns are traditional to Fair Isle knitwear and add a distinctive touch. Rows of shaded diamonds break up the larger patterns and give the impression of many color changes, but only two colors are used in any round. Carry the yarn behind the work as the Shetland knitters do; your socks will be double thickness and warm as toast.

✳ MATERIALS

Yarn

Rowan Pure Wool DK (100% super-wash wool, 137 yards/125m):

1 x 50g (1¾oz) ball, shade 020 Parsley (A)

1 x 50g (1¾oz) ball, shade 021 Glade (B)

1 x 50g (1¾oz) ball, shade 015 Barley (C)

1 x 50g (1¾oz) ball, shade 016 Hessian (D)

1 x 50g (1¾oz) ball, shade 035 Quarry (E)

1 x 50g (1¾oz) ball, shade 007 Cyprus (F)

Needles

Set of four double-pointed needles U.S. size 4/3.5mm

✳ MEASUREMENTS

To fit 8-inch/25cm foot.

Length of leg from bottom of heel: 14 inches/36cm.

Gauge

26 sts and 28 rows measure 4 inches/10cm over pattern using size 4/3.5mm needles (or size needed to obtain correct gauge).

Using A, cast on 64 sts and join, being careful not to twist sts. Arrange sts over three needles (21, 21, 22).

Work rib pattern as follows:

Rounds 1 and 2 (P2A, k2B) rep to end.

Rounds 3 and 4 (P2A, k2C) rep to end.

Rounds 5 and 6 (P2A, k2D) rep to end.

Rounds 7 and 8 (P2A, k2E) rep to end.

Rounds 9 and 10 (P2A, k2F) rep to end.

Rounds 11 and 12 As rounds 7 and 8.

Rounds 13 and 14 As rounds 5 and 6.

Rounds 15 and 16 As rounds 3 and 4.

K 25 rounds foll chart.

Note The pattern repeat does not fit exactly into the number of stitches, so end the pattern and start again at

the beginning of the chart for the new round.

When decreasing, keep the pattern correct after the first 3 sts.

Keeping patt correct, shape leg:

Round 26 K1, k2tog, k to last 3 sts, skp.

Rounds 27–32 Work foll chart.

Rep rounds 26–32 6 more times, finishing on round 60. *50 sts.*

Work even foll chart for 16 more rounds.

Divide for heel:

Slip last 12 sts from third needle onto first needle, and work across 12 st from first needle in heel patt below. *24 sts.*

Divide rem 26 sts onto two needles and leave for instep.

Working in rows, and using B and A alternately, work heel patt as follows:

Row 1 (RS) K2B, k2A.

Row 2 P2B, p2A.

HEEL

Keeping heel patt correct, work 11 more rows on 24 sts on first needle. Turn heel, keeping heel patt correct.

Row 1 K16, skp, turn.

Row 2 P9, p2tog, turn.

Row 3 K10, skp, turn.

Row 4 P11, p2tog, turn.

Cont in this way until all sts are worked onto one needle again. With RS facing k 8 sts in heel patt. *16 sts.*

Slip all instep sts onto one needle.

With spare needle, using B, with RS of work facing, pick up and k 13 sts along side of heel. Break off yarn. Work across instep sts foll chart and keeping patt correct; then, using B, pick up and k 13 sts along left-hand side of heel, k 8 sts from heel. *68 sts.*

SHAPE INSTEP

Round 1 K following chart on all needles.

Round 2 First needle: k to last 3 sts, k2 tog, k1; second needle: k; third needle: k1, skp, k to end.

Rep these two rounds until 52 sts remain.

Work even, foll chart, until round 60 is complete.

SHAPE TOE

Cont working toe in chart patt as follows:

Round 1 First needle: k to last 3 sts, k2tog, k1; second needle: k1, skp, k to last 3 sts, k2tog, k1; third needle: k1, skp, k to end.

Round 2 Knit.

Rep these 2 rounds until 24 sts remain. Place sts from first needle onto end of third needle.

Graft toe sts (see page 142) or bind off tog on the WS.

Make another sock in the same way.

FINISHING

Block or press carefully (see page 143).

Traditional Shetland Pattern Socks

This lovely little pair of socks was designed for us by Jan Ter Heide, a Dutch designer and knitter, who visited the Shetland Islands and found a pair of gloves with this pattern in the Shetland Museum. The small repeating checks are similar to Sanquhar, but are more subtle, and the plain rib has a pretty little mock cable. The yarn is an unusual mixture of merino, a luxury wool, and bamboo, which is soft and absorbent; the finished yarn is silky as well as practical, and is dyed especially for this book in semi-solid dyes that give a lovely soft look. Send for this yarn as a pack direct from Easyknits and you can knit this modern version of an old pattern.

✳ MATERIALS

Yarn

Easyknits (80% pure Merino wool, 20%
bamboo, approx 230 yards/210m):
1 x 50g (1¾oz) hank, Peach Melba (A)
1 x 50g (1¾oz) hank, Bitter Chocolate (B)

Needles

Set of four double-pointed needles U.S.
size 0/2.25mm for both sizes
Set of four double pointed needles U.S.
size 1/2.50mm for both sizes
Set of four double pointed needles U.S.
size 2/2.75mm for second size only

Special Abbreviation

t2r Knit the second stitch on the left-hand
needle, then the first one, then slide them
off the needle together.

✳ MEASUREMENTS

To fit 9–9½ [10–10½]-inch/
23–24 [25–27]cm foot.
Length of leg from bottom of heel:
10 inches/25.5cm.

Gauge

40 sts and 44 rows measure 4 inches/10cm
over pattern using size 1/2.5mm needles
(or size needled to obtain correct gauge).

The ribbing is worked with a mock
cable. Using smallest needles (both
sizes) and yarn B, cast on 68 sts and join
in a round, being careful not to twist
sts. Place a marker at beg of round.
Work 3 rounds in k2, p2 rib.
Round 4 Work mock cable as
follows: *t2r, rep from * to end.
Work 3 more rounds in k2, p2 rib.
Round 8 *t2r, rep from * to end.
Work 3 more rounds in k2, p2 rib.
Round 12 *t2r, rep from * to end.
Work 3 more rounds in k2, p2 rib.
Round 16 *t2r, rep from * to end.
Work 2 more rounds in k2, p2 rib.
Knit 1 round inc 2 sts evenly in
round. *70 sts.*
Change to medium-size needles for
the first size or largest needles for
the second size and work Chart 1
with yarns A and B, repeating 6
more times to complete the round.
Work Chart 2 in the same way.
Rep working Charts 1 and 2
twice more.

HEEL

Using yarn B, change to smallest
needles for the first size; cont
using medium-size needles for
the second size.
Knit the first 30 sts for the heel flap.
Put the next 40 sts on a spare needle
and leave for the instep.
Note Slip the first st purlwise wyib,
so the sts are easy to pick up.
Row 1 Sl 1 p-wise, p to end.
Row 2 Sl 1 p-wise, k to end.
Rep these rows for a total of 30 rows.

Turn heel:
Starting with a p row, p19, p2tog,
turn.
Row 1 Sl 1 p-wise wyib, k9, skp,
turn.
Row 2 Sl 1 p-wise wyif, p9, p2tog,
turn.
Rep rows 1 and 2 until 11 sts
remain, ending with a p row.
Next Row K9, k2tog. *10 sts.*

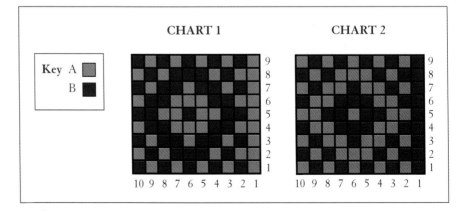

GUSSET

Round 1 First needle: with yarn A pick up and k 16 sts along heel flap; second needle; k 40 sts across instep; third needle, pick up and k 16 sts along heel flap, k10. *82 sts.*

Round 2 First needle: k to last 3 sts, k2tog, k1; second needle: k; third needle, k1, skp, k to end.
Round 3 Knit.
Rep rounds 2 and 3 until 68 sts remain.
Divide these stitches between three needles.

FOOT

Work even using yarn A until foot measures 7¼ [8] inches/18.5 [20]cm from back of heel or 2 inches/5cm less than desired total length.

TOE

Using yarn B, work as follows:
Round 1 First needle: k to last 4 sts, k2tog, k2; second needle: k2, skp, k to last 4 sts, k2tog, k2; third needle: k2, skp, k to end.

Round 2 Knit.
Rep rounds 1 and 2 until 12 sts remain. Rearrange sts on two needles and graft (see page 142) or bind off tog on the WS.

Make another sock in the same way.

FINISHING

Block or press carefully (see page 143).

Argyle

Plaid or tartan leggings or socks, called *cadadh*, were originally made of cloth, which was cut on the bias and sewn together down the back of the leg and under the foot. It is thought that these tartan cloth socks were originated by the clan Campbell of Argyll in Scotland, hence the name Argyle socks. They would have been worn with a kilt, which, in the form that we now know it, was an invention of the 1720s.

Nearly all the elements of Highland dress, including plaid stockings, were preserved by their being adopted by the Highland regiments of the British Army. Ironically, the wearing of tartan by ordinary Scotsmen was banned by the Dress Act—from the battle of Culloden in 1746 until 1782— while at the same time it was being worn as an army uniform; had this not been the case, the kilt, and along with it kilt hose, might have died out.

Less than 50 years later, when George IV visited Scotland in 1822, the kilt became fashionable. Novelist and poet Sir Walter Scott was put in charge of organizing the festivities celebrating the monarch's visit, and laid on a pageant of all the Highlanders and clan chiefs wearing plaid kilts, thereby ensuring it was to become the national dress of Scotland. The King famously had his portrait painted wearing a kilt and plaid kilt hose. Queen Victoria continued the royal patronage of tartan when she visited Scotland and, in 1848, bought Balmoral Castle, where Prince Albert used tartan patterns in the interior design.

It is not known exactly when the appearance of plaid or tartan cloth stockings was copied in knitting, but perhaps in Victorian times. Unlike the colored knitting of Fair Isle, which has small repeating patterns, it was not possible to carry the yarn from one block of color to another, so a separate ball of wool had to be used for each color area. This method of work is called intarsia, and the stockings have to be knitted on two needles instead of four, and have a seam down the back.

The easiest way to plot the color changes in an Argyle pattern is by drawing a chart. Working on two needles, the second and all even-numbered rows have to be read from left to right, and the knitter has the wrong side of the work facing them when these rows are worked. Our Argyle socks in this chapter use charts in the patterns showing all the color changes.

Knitted plaid or Argyle patterns continued to be used as part of Highland dress for pipers and regiments, and in the 1920s they became fashionable wear for golfers. Argyle sweaters, hats, and knee-high socks were all worn on the golf course and are still part of traditional golfing attire today.

The pattern has more recently become associated with fine cashmere knitting from the mills in the Scottish Borders. This type of knitwear has gone through waves of popularity in the 1940s and 1950s, and has taken an enduring hold in the fashions of young and old alike. In fact, it has hardly ever been completely out of fashion, and it seems to be popular with knitters, and men and women who wear this design, well up to the present day.

Men's Argyle Knee-Length Socks

Here, Argyle has been used on knee-length men's socks, knitted appropriately in a Scottish tweed wool—the names of the colors of which are reminiscent of the islands of Scotland and the Highland landscape. The socks are knitted on two needles with the intarsia method, and the charts make it easy to follow the pattern—but make sure you create a nice, flat seam for the comfort of the wearer. This design, with the turnover cuff, which hides a plain rib, is close to the traditional Argyle sock, which would have been worn with a kilt, but it has plenty of other uses as well, and will be sure to invite admiring glances whenever it is seen.

✳ MATERIALS

Yarn

Rowan Scottish Tweed 4-ply (100% pure
new wool, 120 yards/110m):

4 x 25g (approx 1oz) balls, shade 00007
Lewis Grey (A)

2 x 25g (approx 1oz) balls, shade 00022
Celtic Mix (B)

2 x 25g (approx 1oz) balls, shade 00027
Blue Mist (C)

2 x 25g (approx 1oz) balls, shade 00017
Lobster (D)

1 x 25g (approx 1oz) ball, shade 00018
Thatch (E)

Ncedles

One pair U.S. size 2/3mm knitting needles
One pair U.S. size 3/3.25mm knitting
needles

✳ MEASUREMENTS

To fit 10–10½-inch/25–27cm foot.
Length of leg from bottom of heel
(cuff folded): 18 inches/46cm.

Gauge

24 sts and 36 rows measure 4 inches/10cm
using size 3/3.25mm needles (or size
needed to obtain correct gauge). Note:
These socks were knitted with metric
needles; if you have trouble achieving the
correct gauge, try using metric needles.

CUFF

Using larger needles, cast on
68 sts as follows:
1 E, 15 C, 2 D, 15 A, 2 E, 15 A,
2 B, 15 C, 1 E.
Follow Chart A: 32 rows.
Read odd-numbered (knit)
rows from right to left and
even-numbered (purl) rows
from left to right.

LEG

Change to smaller needles and,
using A, work in k1, p1 rib for 31
rows, ending with the WS of the
cuff facing.
Change to larger needles. Beg with
a k row follow chart B from row
1–130, again reading odd-numbered
(k) rows from right to left and even-
numbered (p) rows from left to right.

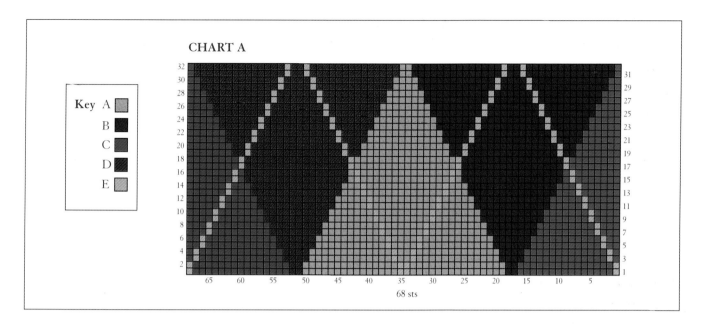

CHART A

Key A
B
C
D
E

68 sts

HEEL

**Row 1 Using A, sl 1, k17, over
the first 18 sts: place rem 50 sts
on a stitch holder for the instep.
Row 2 Purl.
Row 3 Sl 1, k17.
Row 4 Purl.
Rep rows 3 and 4 on the 18 heel sts
until 16 rows in all have been
worked ending with a purl row.**

Turn heel:
Row 1 K2, k2tog, k1, turn.
Row 2 Sl 1, p3, turn.
Row 3 K3, k2tog, k1, turn.
Row 4 Sl 1, p4, turn.
Row 5 K4, k2tog, k1, turn.
Row 6 Sl 1, p5, turn.
Cont working as given above until
all sts are worked ending with k9,

k2tog. *10 sts*.
Pick up and k 11 sts on side of heel.
Place the 50 sts from stitch holder
onto left-hand needle and work
across 32 sts of the 50 sts as follows:
14 A, 1 E, 2 A, 1 E, 14 A.
On the rem 18 sts cont as given
for first half of heel from ** to **,
ending with a k row.

Turn heel:
Row 1 P2, p2tog, p1, turn.
Row 2 Sl 1, k3, turn.
Row 3 P3, p2tog, k1, turn.
Row 4 Sl 1, k4, turn.
Row 5 P4, p2tog, k1, turn.
Row 6 Sl 1, k5, turn.
Cont working as given above until
all sts are worked, ending with p9,
p2tog. *10 sts*.
Pick up and p 11 sts on side of heel.

Place the sts from stitch holder onto
left-hand needle and purl across
row with A on A stitches, and E
on E stitches. *74 sts*.

SHAPE INSTEP

Using Chart C, work as follows:
Row 1 Using A, k18, k2tog, k1,
follow Chart C for 32 sts. Using A,
k1, skp, k to end.
Row 2 Purl with same colors.
Row 3 Using A, k17, k2tog, k1,
follow Chart C for 32 sts. Using A,
k1, skp, k to end.
Row 4 Purl with same colors.
Row 5 Using A, k16, k2tog, k3,
follow Chart C for 28 sts. Using A,
k1, skp, k to end.
Cont to dec as above, keeping A at
the sides and following Chart C

CHART B

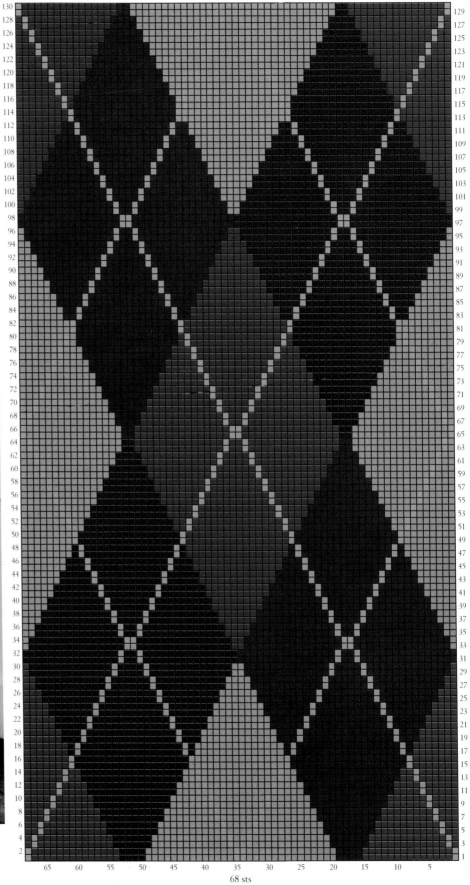

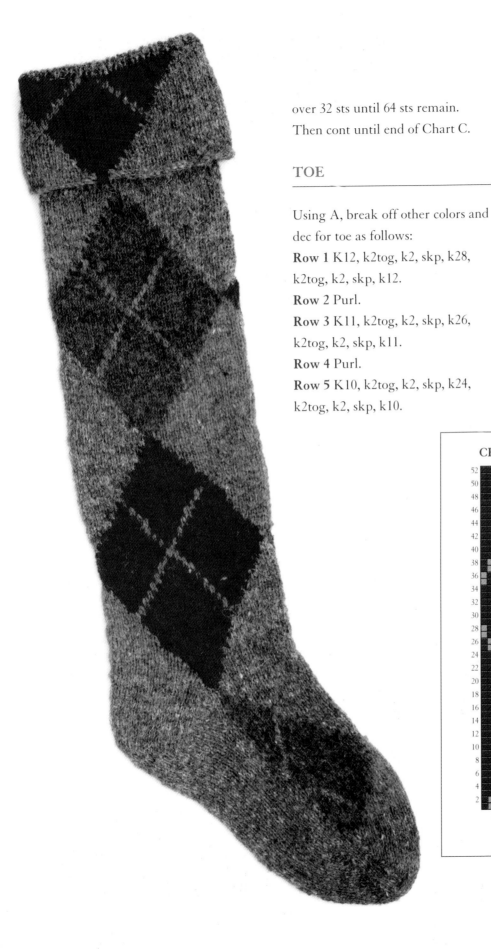

over 32 sts until 64 sts remain. Then cont until end of Chart C.

TOE

Using A, break off other colors and dec for toe as follows:

Row 1 K12, k2tog, k2, skp, k28, k2tog, k2, skp, k12.

Row 2 Purl.

Row 3 K11, k2tog, k2, skp, k26, k2tog, k2, skp, k11.

Row 4 Purl.

Row 5 K10, k2tog, k2, skp, k24, k2tog, k2, skp, k10.

Cont to dec as given above until 20 sts remain.

Divide sts evenly between two needles. Graft (see page 142) or bind off tog both sets of sts on the WS.

Make another sock in the same way.

FINISHING

Join leg and foot seams (see page 141) and darn in ends on the WS. Block or press carefully (see page 143).

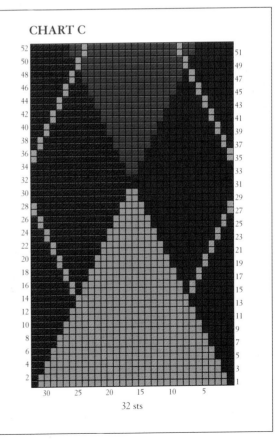

CHART C

32 sts

Argyle Over-the-Knee Socks

These stylish over-the-knee socks show just how adaptable Argyle patterns can be. A far cry from Highland dress, these can be worn over tights, leggings, or skinny jeans, as well as on their own. The pastel pink and deep raspberry will complement many of the colors in your wardrobe, and the finished look is both fun and sporty. The pattern is confined to the front of the socks, so that the leg can be shaped properly to fit. As usual with Argyle, intarsia knitting is used and the sock has a seam at the back of the leg and the sides of the foot.

✳ MATERIALS

Yarn

Rowan Pure Wool 4-ply (100% super-
wash wool, 174 yards/160m):

2 x 50g (1¾oz) balls, shade 449 Vintage (A)

1 x 50g (1¾oz) ball, shade 412 Snow (B)

2 x 50g (1¾oz) balls, shade 428
Raspberry (C)

1 x 50g (1¾oz) ball, shade 401 Clay (D)

Needles

One pair U.S. size 3/3.25mm needles
One pair U.S. size 5/3.75mm needles
Set of four double-pointed needles
U.S. size 5/3.75mm

✳ MEASUREMENTS

To fit 9 [10]-inch/23 [25.5]cm foot.
Length of leg from bottom of heel:
21 inches/53cm.

Gauge

28 sts and 36 rows measure 4 inches/10cm
over St st and Argyle pattern using size
3/3.25mm needles (or size needed to
obtain correct gauge).

SPECIAL INSTRUCTIONS

The chart panel is knitted using the intarsia method (see page 141). For this, each individual diamond is worked using a separate length of yarn, and several lengths of white are used for the diagonals.

Using a pair of larger needles and doubled yarn, cast on 91 sts in A. Break off 1 strand of yarn and continue with a single strand throughout.

Change to smaller needles and purl 1 row (this is the RS).

Next row K2, (p3, k3) to last 5 sts, p3, k2.

Cont in rib as now set for a total of 2 inches/5cm.

Change to larger needles and work from chart with side panels in A, set as follows:

Row 1 K21 C, work row 1 of chart over center 49 sts, k21 C.

Row 2 P21 C, work row 2 of chart over center 49 sts, p21 C.

Work 8 more rows in patt as set, then dec in solid-color section as follows: K18, k2tog, k1, work from chart, k1, skp, k to end.

Cont as set, dec as above on every foll 8th row to 71 sts, then on every 6th row to 55 sts (there will now be 3 sts in A at each side of the 49 chart sts).

DIVIDE FOR HEEL & INSTEP

Next row Leave first 14 sts on a stitch holder, patt 27 from chart, turn.

Cont on these 27 sts in patt for 3 full triangles [for the larger size work 7 more rows finishing with the diagonals in B].

Both sizes Work 1 row in C and leave on stitch holder.

With right sides facing and seam at center back, slip rem 28 sts onto one needle.

Join in C and knit 1 row, dec 1 st at center. *27 sts.*

Cont in St st for 24 rows, always slipping the first st of each row.

Turn heel:

Continuing in C work as follows:

Row 1 K17, skp, turn.

Row 2 Sl 1, p7, p2tog, turn.

Row 3 Sl 1, k7, ssk, turn.

Row 4 As row 2.

Rep rows 3 and 4 until 9 sts remain. Break yarn and leave sts on a stitch holder. Join yarn to beg of heel, pick up and k 14 sts along right side of heel flap, k 9 from stitch holder, pick up and k 14 sts along left side of heel flap. *37 sts.*

Next row Purl.

SHAPE SOLE

Now cont in St st and shape as follows:

Row 1 K2, skp, k to last 4 sts, k2tog, k2.

Row 2 K1, p to last st, k1.

Rep last 2 rows until 27 sts remain, then cont in St st until sole section measures same as top section, ending with a WS row.

Next row Divide all sts over three double-pointed needles: first needle 13 sts; second needle 27 sts; third needle 14 sts.

SHAPE TOE

Round 1 First needle: k to last 3 sts, k2 tog, k1; second needle: k1, ssk, k to last 3 sts, k2tog, k1; third needle: k1, ssk, k to end.

Round 2 and every alt round Knit.

Cont to dec in this way on alt rounds until 26 sts remain, then dec as on round 1 on foll round. *22 sts.* Graft (see page 142 or bind off sts tog on the WS.

Make another sock in the same way.

FINISHING

Darn loose ends back into their own colors. Join the seams at the side of the foot and at the back of the leg (see page 141). Block or press carefully (see page 143).

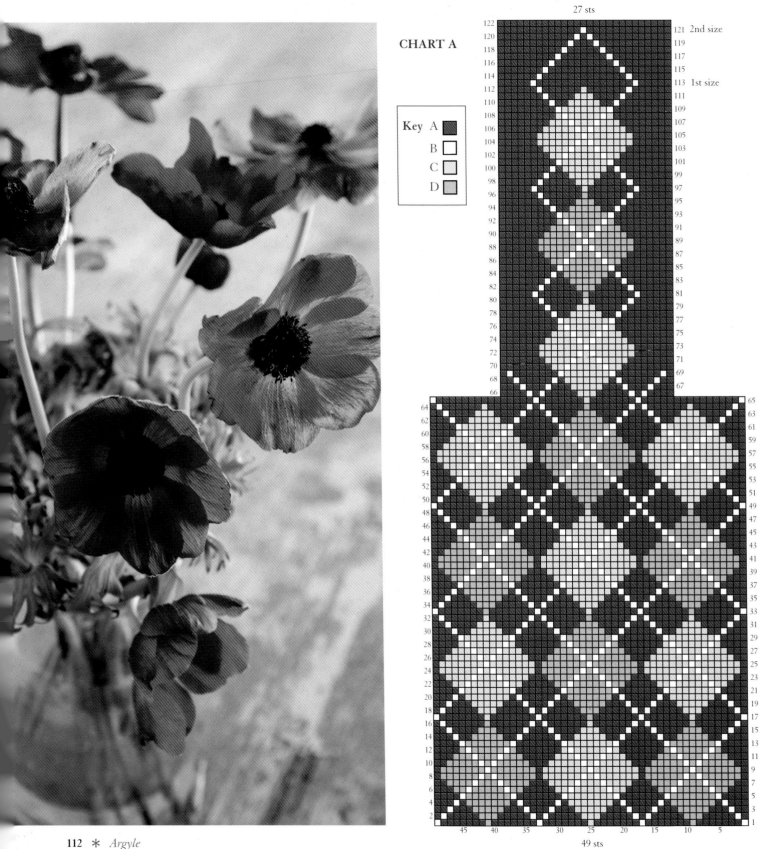

CHART A

Key A
     B
     C
     D

27 sts

49 sts

Men's Argyle Socks

These Argyle socks can be knitted in men's or women's sizes and are versatile enough to wear in the town and country alike. The pattern takes you back to the 1940s but is also fashionably up-to-date, making these socks traditional enough for a man to wear with a suit to the city, and witty enough for a girl to wear with just about anything. The wool is super-wash 4-ply, which makes the socks extremely easy to care for. What more could you ask of a single pair of socks?

✳ MATERIALS

Yarn

Rowan Pure Wool 4-Ply (100% super-
wash wool, 174 yards/160m):
2 x 50g (1¾oz) balls, shade 411 Navy (A)
1 x 50g (1¾oz) ball, shade 402 Shale (B)
1 x 50g (1¾oz) ball, shade 428
Raspberry (C)

Needles

One pair U.S. size 2/2.75mm needles

✳ MEASUREMENTS

To fit 10½-inch/27cm foot (adjustable).
Length of leg from bottom of heel:
10¼ inches/26cm.

Gauge

30 sts and 42 rows measure 4 inches/10cm
using size 2/2.75mm needles (or size
needed to obtain correct gauge).

✳ NOTE

Be sure to twist yarns when changing
colors, to avoid making a hole. Before
starting, break off two lengths each of B
and C of about 2 yards/2m each to use for
the narrow diagonals; these sts are in **bold**.

Using A cast on 70 sts.
Work in rows:
Row 1 K1, (p2, k2) to last st, k1.
Row 2 P1, (p2, k2) to last st, p1.
Rep these 2 rows for a total of
2 inches/5cm.

Now foll chart, working all k rows
from right to left, and all p rows
from left to right, until row 66 has
been worked. Or follow the written
instructions below.
Row 1 K 2 B, 15 A, **1 C**, **1 B**, 15 A, 2
C, 15 A, **1 B**, **1 C**, 15 A, 2 B.
Row 2 Purl using same colors (chart
rows 1 and 2).
Cont as above, adding 1 more st in
color to the B half-diamonds on
each end of every k row, purl using
same colors; add 2 more sts to the
center C diamond; working 1 st less
in color on each side of the 2 A
diamonds every k row, moving the
C diagonals 1 st toward the outside
and the B diagonals 1 st toward the
center on every k row, until the first
crossing of diagonals into adjoining
colors (chart rows 17 and 18).

Cont working as above until row
32 has been completed. On the next
row the B diagonals will cross in the
center of the C diamond.

Cont in patt, working 1 st less
in color at each side of the
center C diamond and
1 st in each B diamond,
every other row,
until diagonals cross
into adjoining colors
again (chart rows
49 and 50).

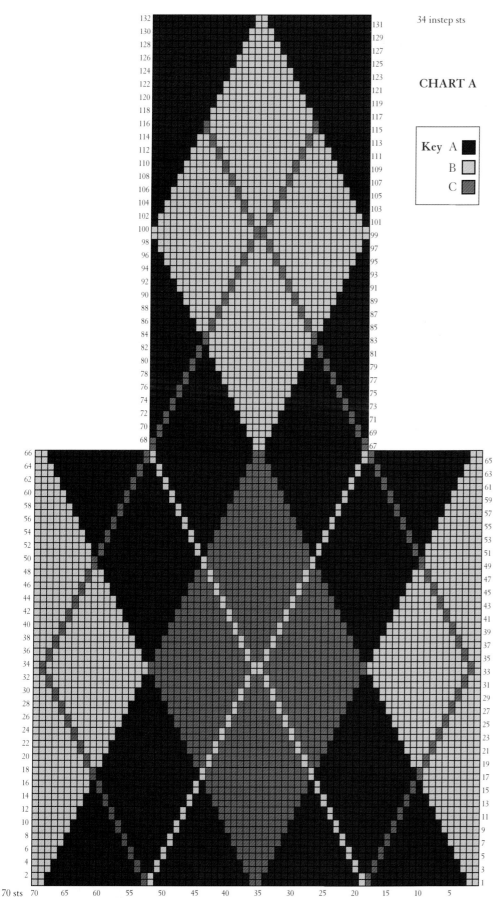

CHART A

Key A ■
B ▢
C ▨

Cont in patt until the center C diamond has been completed. This ends the first half of the chart at row 66.

Break off the B and center C balls of yarn and the 2 B strands.

HEEL

Row 1 Using B, sl 1, k1, over the first 18 sts; place rem 52 sts on a stitch holder or spare needle.
Row 2 Purl.
Rep these 2 rows on the 18 heel sts until 32 rows in all have been worked, ending with a p row. Turn this half of heel as follows:
Row 1 K2, k2tog, k1, turn.
Row 2 Sl 1, p3, turn.
Row 3 K3, k2tog, k1, turn.
Row 4 Sl 1, p4, turn.
Row 5 K4, k2tog, k1, turn.
Row 6 Sl 1, p5, turn.
Cont working as given above until all sts are worked; there will be 10 sts on the needle, ending with k9, k2tog.

Pick up and k 17 sts (15 and 2 in the corner) on the side of the heel. Place the sts from the stitch holder on the left-hand needle and foll chart for foot. Or work in patt across the 34 instep sts as follows:

Next row k 1 C, 15 A, 2 B, 15 A, 1 C (chart row 67). Place the 61 sts just worked on a stitch holder. Reversing shaping, work as given for first half of heel on rem 18 sts for 33 rows, ending with a "sl 1, k1" row. Turn this half of heel as follows:

Row 1 P2, p2tog, p1, turn.

Row 2 Sl 1, k3, turn.

Row 3 P3, p2tog, p1, turn.

Row 4 Sl 1, k4, turn.

Row 5 P4, p2tog, p1, turn.

Row 6 Sl 1, k5, turn.

Cont working as given above until all sts have been worked; there will be 10 sts on the needle, ending with p9, p2tog.

Pick up and p 17 sts on side of heel. Place the sts from stitch holder onto left-hand needle and p across row with same colors for 44 sts. K last 27 sts in A. *88 sts.*

SHAPE INSTEP

Row 1 Using A, k25, k2tog, k1, then k **1 C**, 13 A, 4 B, 13 A, **1 C**, change to A and k1, skp, k25.

Row 2 and all even rows P using same colors.

Row 3 Using A, k24, k2tog, k2, then k **1 C**, 11 A, 6 B, 11 A, **1 C**, change to A and k2, skp, k24 (chart row 71).

Row 5 Using A, k23, k2tog, k3, then k **1 C**, 9 A, 8 B, 9 A, **1 C**, change to A and k3, skp, k23 (chart row 73).

Cont to dec in this way, adding 1 more st in color to each side of the B diamond across instep, moving the C diagonals 1 st toward the center on every k row, until 70 sts remain. Work even on the 70 sts until sts on the needle are as follows: 18 A, 16 B, **2 C**, 16 B, 18 A (chart row 99). At this point the C diagonals will cross each other. Purl using same colors, cont in patt working 1 st less in color on each side of the B diamond; moving the C diagonals 1 st outward, every k row, until sts are on the needle as follows: 26 A, **1 C**, 16 B, **1 C**, 26 A (chart row 115). Purl using same colors.

Break off both strands of C and cont in patt working 1 st less in color on each side of the B diamond, every k row, until diamond has been completed (there will be 2 B sts in the center of last p row [chart row 132]). Work in St st using A only for ¾ inch/2cm, for 10½-inch/27cm foot, or until foot measures 2 inches/5cm less than desired length, measuring from back of heel.

DECREASE FOR TOE

Row 1 Using B, k15, k2tog, k2, skp, k28, k2tog, k2, skp, k15.

Row 2 and all even-numbered rows Purl.

Row 3 K14, k2tog, k2, skp, k26, k2tog, k2, skp, k14.

Row 5 K13, k2tog, k2, skp, k24, k2tog, k2; skp, k13.

Cont to dec as given above until 26 sts remain.

Divide the sts between two needles and graft (see page 142) or bind off tog on the WS.

Make another sock in the same way.

FINISHING

Join leg and foot seams (see page 143). Block or press carefully (see page 143).

Lace Knitting

Openwork stitches are found worked in Aran sweaters and fishermen's ganseys, but the complex lace patterns of the British Isles are mainly associated with the Shetland Islands. There was certainly lace knitting in other parts of Europe before it developed in Shetland, particularly in Russia and Spain, and these patterns would have reached Shetland by the sea trading routes. By the 1840s Shetland knitters were starting to knit lace shawls from very fine hand-spun wool, and these were being sold in London.

The northern Shetland Isle of Unst became the home of the finest spinning, and the shawls produced there were famous for being so delicate that they could be drawn through a wedding ring. There were many hand-knitted lace articles in the Great Exhibition of 1851, held in the Crystal Palace in London's Hyde Park, and some had also been presented to Queen Victoria. This ensured that lace shawls, stockings, and other items had a ready market in the south of England, and knitting became one of the mainstays of the economy of the Shetland Islands.

Taking their knitwear to market was very important for knitters and a remarkable tale of Shetland endurance stems from this period. In 1886 60-year-old Betty Mouat boarded a fishing boat to take her knitting to Lerwick to sell. A storm blew up suddenly and the unfortunate skipper was washed overboard; the mate and the deckhand attempted his rescue by launching the small dinghy, but by the time they had given up the search they realized the boat, with Betty alone on board, was sailing faster than they could row. They were able to make landfall to alert rescuers, but boats searched for two days and could find no trace of Betty. Amazingly, after nine days at sea, the boat was washed ashore in Norway and she was rescued alive. She returned home a celebrity, and Queen Victoria herself sent her £20.

As well as the fine lace shawls, the Shetland women also knitted *haps*, or shawls, which they wore while working. These were plain garter stitch in the center with an openwork wave pattern in the border, often striped with natural or dyed colors like the one on page 87. When doubled across the diagonal, the pointed ends could be crossed over the body and tied behind the back, leaving the hands free for the women to knit even as they carried the peat back to the crofts on their backs.

By the early twentieth century lace production was nearly all mechanized and had its base in Nottingham, in the north of England, but when the Second World War broke out the lace factories were taken over for the production of munitions. This fact, along with the arrival of servicemen in Shetland, revived the cottage industry. Lace sweaters and scarves would be bought by soldiers and sailors for their wives and girlfriends, and remain an enduring picture of the fashion of that time. Lace wool stockings were also knitted in the 1940s by home knitters who could not obtain silk stockings. Vintage knitting patterns show the popularity of hand-knitted lace, for pullovers and cardigans as well as shawls and stockings, and can be a source of inspiration to today's knitters.

Diamond Panel Socks with Lacy Cuffs

If you want to keep your toes warm on an autumn evening, there is nothing nicer than the feel of this merino wool and cashmere blend on your feet. The lacy diamond design, which gives these socks a pretty 1930s look, is taken from a vintage pattern for a pair of bed socks. We have added a cuff for a lacy finishing touch, which gives the socks an extra-feminine feel and means they work well with pretty floral prints and high heels. For people who find knitting on four needles difficult, these socks are easy to knit in 4-ply yarn on two needles and can be sewn up afterward.

✳ MATERIALS

Yarn

Rowan Cashsoft 4-ply (57% extra-fine merino, 33% acrylic microfiber, 10% cashmere, 197 yards/180m): 2 x 50g (1¾ oz) balls, shade 426 Mosaic

Needles

One pair U.S. size 3/3.25mm needles

✳ MEASUREMENTS

To fit 9–9½–inch/23–24cm foot.

Length of leg from bottom of heel (cuff folded): 6½ inches/16.5cm.

Gauge

28 sts and 36 rows measure 4 inches/10cm using size 3/3.25mm needles (or size needed to obtain correct gauge).

Cast on 55 sts. Work in k1, p2 rib for 1½ inches/4cm. Work in St st for 1½ inches/4cm.

DIAMOND PANEL

Row 1 K27, yo, k2tog tbl, k26.
Row 2 and alt rows K1, p to last st, k1.
Row 3 K25, k2tog, yo, k1, yo, k2tog tbl, k25.
Row 5 K24, k2tog, yo, k3, yo, k2tog tbl, k24.
Row 7 K23, (k2tog, yo) twice, k1, (yo, k2tog tbl) twice, k23.
Row 9 K22, (k2tog, yo) twice, k3, (yo, k2tog tbl) twice, k22.
Row 11 K24, yo, k2tog tbl, yo, sk2p, yo, k2tog, yo, k24.
Row 13 K25, yo, k2tog tbl, k1, k2tog, yo, k25.
Row 15 K26, yo, sk2p, yo, k26.
Row 16 K1, p to last st, k1.
Rows 5–16 form the diamond panel.
Work 2 rows St st.

INSTEP

Keeping diamond patt correct, work as follows:
Row 1 K23, (k2tog, yo) twice, k1, (yo, k2tog tbl) twice, k9.
Slip rem 14 sts and first 14 sts of row onto a piece of scrap yarn. Noting that 14 fewer sts will be worked in St st at both ends of needle, cont to work diamond panel as at beg, starting with row 9. Cont until 5 diamonds in all have been worked, finishing with row 16 of panel.
Next row K13, yo, k2tog, k12.
Cont in St st until work measures 6 inches/15cm (for a 9½-inch/24cm foot) from where sts were divided, finishing at the end of a p row.

SHAPE TOE

Row 1 K1, k2tog tbl, k to last 3 sts, k2tog, k1.
Row 2 K1, p to last st, k1.
Rep these 2 rows 7 more times.
Slip rem 11 sts onto a piece of yarn.

HEEL

Slip groups of 14 sts onto one needle, placing open edges tog. With RS facing, join yarn and work as follows on the 28 sts on needle:
Row 1 Sl 1, k to last st, turn.
Row 2 Sl 1, p to last st, turn.
Row 3 Sl 1, k to last 2 sts, turn.
Row 4 Sl 1, p to last 2 sts, turn.
Cont in this way working 1 st less on every row until the row "Sl 1, p to last 9 sts, turn" has been worked.
Next row Sl 1, k to last 8 sts, turn.
Next row Sl 1, p to last 8 sts, turn.
Next row Sl 1, k to last 7 sts, turn.

Next row Sl 1, p to last 7 sts, turn.
Cont in this way working 1 more
st on every row until all sts are
worked onto one needle again.
Cont in St st until work measures
same as first half up to toe shaping,
dec 1 st at end of last row. *27 sts.*
Shape toe as for first half, then graft
the two groups of sts tog (see page 142).

CUFF

With WS facing, pick up and k 56
sts from cuff edge.
Knit next WS row to form a ridge.
Next row K, inc to 71 as follows: k2,
(M1, k4) 5 times; (M1, k3) 4 times;
(M1, k4) 5 times; M1, k2.
Begin pattern as follows:
Row 1 Knit.
Row 2 (K3, yf, k3tog, yf, k1) to last
st, k1.
Row 3 Knit.
Row 4 (K2, yf, k1, k3tog, k1, yf) to
last st, k1.
Rep these 4 rows until cuff covers
rib and the first 1 inch/2.5cm of St st.
Knit 3 rows, bind off loosely.

Make another sock in the same way.

FINISHING

Block or press carefully (see page 143).
Using a flat seam join side and back
seams (see page 143). Press seams.

Lacy Knee-Length Socks

These are reminiscent of the lacy stockings of the 1940s—and that is not surprising, as that is exactly where this stitch was found. We have made the original vintage pattern into a more useful length, with the same beautifully shaped leg with a seam at the back—the socks can be worn pulled up to the knee or slouched down around the calf. Knitted here in a 4-ply Scottish tweed wool, the socks would be even more luxurious in a cashmere blend of the same weight. They look good on lots of occasions, from country walks across the fields or beach to days in the city.

✳ MATERIALS

Yarn

Rowan Scottish Tweed 4-ply (100% pure new wool, 120 yards/110m): 6 x 25g (approx 1 oz) balls, shade 6 Sea Green

Needles

One pair U.S. size 1/2.25mm needles
One pair U.S. size 2/2.75mm needles
Set of four double-pointed needles U.S. size 2/2.75mm

✳ MEASUREMENTS

To fit 8½–9-inch/22–23cm foot.
Length of leg from bottom of heel: 16 inches/41cm.
Width of sock across fullest part: 6 inches/15cm.

Gauge

36 sts and 46 rows measure 4 inches/10cm using size 2/2.75mm needles (or size needed to obtain correct gauge).

Using smaller needles, cast on 89 sts. Work 2 inches/5cm in k1, p1 rib, finishing with the WS facing.
Next row (Rib 3, M1) twice, (rib 4, M1) 9 times, rib 5, M1, (rib 4, M1) 9 times, rib 3, M1, rib 3.
Change to larger needles.

PATTERN

Row 1 K1, *p1, k1, p5, k1, p1, k1, rep from * to end.
Row 2 P1, *k1, p1, k5, p1, k1, p1, rep from * to end.
Row 3 As row 1.
Row 4 As row 2.
Row 5 K1, *p1, yo, skp, p3, k2tog, yo, p1, k1, rep from * to end.
Row 6 P1, *k2, p1, k3, p1, k2, p1, rep from * to end.
Row 7 K1, *p2, yo, skp, p1, k2tog, yo, p2, k1, rep from * to end.
Row 8 K4, *p1, k1, p1, k3, p1, k3, rep from * to last 7 sts, p1, k1, p1, k4.
Row 9 K1, *p3, yo, skp, yo, p3, k1, rep from * to end.
Row 10 K5, p1, *k4, p1, rep from * to last 5 sts, k5.
These 10 rows form the pattern.
Cont in patt, dec at each end of next and every foll 6th row until there are 89 sts, and then at each end of every foll 4th row until there are 71 sts.

Work even until piece measures 13¾ inches/35cm from cast-on edge, ending with a RS row and leaving last 16 sts unworked.

HEEL

Move last 39 instep sts to holder and slip the first and last 16 sts of the row onto a larger needlefor heel, with outer edges of work in center to form back seam. *32 sts.*
Work backward and forward for 30 rows as follows:
Row 1 *K1, sl 1, rep from * to last st, k1.
Row 2 Purl.

Turn heel:
Next row K16, skp, k1, turn; p5, p2tog, p1, turn; k6, skp, k1, turn. Cont in this way until all sts are worked. *18 sts.*
Now with front of work facing, k to end of needle, pick up and k 17 sts up side of heel, turn, p back picking up and purling 17 sts up other side of heel. *52 sts.*
Work 2 rows in St st.
Next row K2, skp, k to last 4 sts, k2tog, k2.
Next row Purl.
Rep these 2 rows until 30 sts remain. Work even in St st until foot measures 5 inches/13cm or 2 inches/5cm less than desired length, leaving these sts on a spare needle.

INSTEP

Return to instep sts and work backward and forward in patt until

work measures same length as foot. Now put all sts on three larger double-pointed needles and work 1 inch/2.5cm in St st.
Now divide sts so that you have 35 across center of foot on first needle, next 17 on second needle, and 17 on third needle. *69 sts.*
Next round First needle: k1, skp, k to last 3 sts, k2tog, k1; second needle: k1, skp, k to end; third needle: k to last 3 sts, k2tog, k1.
Next round Knit.
Rep these 2 rounds until 21 sts remain, then work 1 round more,

decreasing at the end of the second needle only. *20 sts.*

Place 5 sts from second needle and 5 sts from third needle onto one needle. Graft (see page 142) or bind off these sts on the WS tog with 10 sts from first needle.

Make another sock in the same way.

FINISHING

Block or press carefully (see page 143). Using a flat seam, join leg and foot seams (see page 143). Press seams.

Over-the-Knee Lacy Stockings

Hand-knitted stockings were popular in the 1940s before nylon stockings could be bought, and these take us back to that era. We have used the traditional Shetland lace eyelet pattern, as used for the cardigan in my previous book, *Country Weekend Knits*, but have changed the yarn to a merino wool, worsted spun with a tight twist, making the knitting very elastic and with good stitch definition. Conveniently, this particular yarn can also be machine-washed and dried, which would be the envy of a knitter from the past. The lacy pattern will show up to best advantage when carefully blocked after washing.

✳ MATERIALS

Yarn

Louet Gems Fingering Weight 4-ply
(100% merino wool, 185 yards/169m):
4 x 50g (1¾ oz) balls, shade 43 Pewter

Needles

Set of four double-pointed needles
U.S. size 3/3.25mm

✳ MEASUREMENTS

To fit 9-inch/23cm foot (adjustable).
Length of leg from bottom of heel:
27 inches/69cm.

Gauge

28 sts and 40 rows measure 4 inches/10cm
using size 3/3.25mm needles (or size
needed to obtain correct gauge).

Cast on 84 sts loosely and join, being careful not to twist sts. Divide sts evenly between three needles. Knit in rounds of k2, p2 rib for 3 inches/7.5cm.

PATTERN

Round 1 *K1, yo, k1, k3tog, k1, yo, k1, rep from * to end.
Round 2 K to end.
Round 3 *K2, yo, k3tog, yo, k2, rep from * to end.
Round 4 K to end.
These 4 rounds form the patt.
Work another 8 rounds in patt.

Keeping patt correct, dec 1 st at each end of next and every foll 14th round until there are 64 sts; then at each end of every 8th round until there are 56 sts. Work even until the work measures 22½ inches/57cm.

Turn heel:
Next row K13, turn.
Next row P26, turn.
Leave rem 30 sts on a spare needle for instep.
On these 26 sts, work as follows:
Row 1 (K1, sl 1) to end.
Row 2 Purl to end.
Rep these 2 rows 9 more times.
Now work as follows:
Row 1 K12, skp, k1, turn.
Row 2 P1, p2tog, p1, turn.

Row 3 K2, skp, k1, turn.

Row 4 P3, p2tog, p1, turn.

Row 5 K4, skp, k1, turn.

Row 6 P5, p2tog, p1, turn.

Row 7 K6, skp, k1, turn.

Row 8 P7, p2tog, p1, turn.

Row 9 K8, skp, k1, turn.

Row 10 P9, p2tog, p1, turn.

Row 11 K10, skp, k1, turn.

Row 12 P11, p2tog, p1, turn.

Next row With RS facing, k 14 sts across needle, pick up and k 11 sts up side of heel, turn.

P to end of needle, pick up and k 11 sts up side of heel, turn. *36 sts.* Work 2 rows in St st.

Next row K2, skp, k to last 4 sts, k2tog, k2.

Next row P to end.

Rep these 2 rows until 22 sts remain. Work even in St st until foot measures 6 inches/15cm for a 9-inch/23cm foot, or longer as required. Leave these sts on a spare needle.

INSTEP

Return to 30 instep sts on the spare needle and work as follows:

Row 1 K1, *k1, yo, k1, k3tog, k1, yo, k1, rep from * to last st, k1.

Row 2 Purl to end.

Row 3 K1, *k2, yo, k3tog, yo, k2, rep from * to last st, k1.

Row 4 Purl to end.

Work even in patt until piece is the same length as bottom of foot.

Put all sts (52) on three needles. Working in rounds, work 1 inch/ 2.5cm in St st.

Divide the sts so you have 26 sts on the first needle, across top of foot, and 13 sts on the other two needles.

Next round First needle: k1, skp, k to last 3 sts, k2tog, k1; second needle: k1, skp, k to end of needle; third needle, k to last 3 sts, k2tog, k1.

Next round Knit.

Rep these 2 rounds until 16 sts remain. Place sts from second and third needles on one needle and graft (see page 142) or bind off the two sets of stitches tog.

Make another stocking in the same way.

FINISHING

Join foot seams (see page 143). Block or press carefully (see page 143).

Falling Leaves Lacy Socks

These socks are definitely for summer—the vibrant green cotton yarn and the openwork stitch, in a pattern called Falling Leaves, makes one think of summer clothes in bright, crisp cottons. The picot hem at the top of the socks adds a pretty finishing touch, and the lacy pattern continues down the top of the foot. The cotton yarn used here is mercerized to give it a lustrous sheen and a good stitch definition. The weight is between a double-knitting and a 4-ply, so if you want to use another yarn, check your gauge carefully and change your needle size if necessary.

* MATERIALS

Yarn

Rowan Cotton Glace (100% cotton, 126 yards/115m): 3 x 50g (1¾oz) balls, shade 812 Ivy

Needles

Set of four double-pointed needles U.S. size 2/2.75mm

Set of four double-pointed needles U.S. size 3/3mm

Special Abbreviation

slpn *Slip last stitch of previous needle.*

* MEASUREMENTS

To fit 8½ [9, 9½]-inch/21.5 [23, 24]cm foot. Length of leg from bottom of heel: 10 inches/25cm.

Gauge

26 sts and 38 rows measure 4 inches/10cm using size 2/2.75mm needles (or size needed to obtain correct gauge. Note: These socks were knitted with metric needles; if you have trouble achieving the correct gauge, try using metric needles.

Note It is a good idea to work at least one pattern repeat before beginning the socks to familiarize yourself with how it is formed; cast on 21 sts and work rows 9–24 of instep.

Using smaller needles, cast on 58 sts and join, being careful not to twist sts. Knit 8 rounds.
Next round K1 (yo, k2tog) to last st, k1. Knit 9 rounds.
Turn hem to make picot edge by * knitting 1 st from cast-on round with one from needle.

Knit next st on needle skipping 1 from the cast-on round.
Rep from * to end, inc in last st. (Skipping every other st in this way helps to make the hem lie flatter, but be careful to pick up the correct corresponding st from the cast-on round or the hem will be distorted.)

Change to larger needles and k 1 round, increasing 2 sts evenly around. *60 sts.*
Continue in Falling Leaves pattern as follows. Move the sts around the needles if necessary to make it easier to work, but keep a marker at the beginning of the original round.

FALLING LEAVES PATTERN

Round 1 (K1, yo, k3, sk2p, k3, yo) to end.
Round 2 and every foll even-numbered round Knit.
Round 3 (K2, yo, k2, sk2p, k2, yo, k1) to end.
Round 5 (K3, yo, k1, sk2p, k1, yo, k2) to end.
Round 7 (K4, yo, sk2p, yo, k3) to end.
Round 9 (Slpn, k2tog, psso, k3, yo, k1, yo, k3, sk2p, k3, yo, k1, yo, k3) to end.
Round 11 (Slpn, k2tog, psso, k2, yo, k3, yo, k2, sk2p, k2, yo, k3, yo, k2) to end.

Round 13 (Slpn, k2tog, psso, k1, yo, k5, yo, k1, sk2p, k1, yo, k5, yo, k1) to end.

Round 15 (Slpn, k2tog, psso, yo, k7, yo, sk2p, yo, k7, yo) to end.

Round 16 Knit.

Rep rounds 1–16 once more, then rounds 1–7 again.

Change to smaller needles and work rounds 8–16, then rounds 1–7 again.

HEEL

K 16, slip last 15 sts of round onto end of same needle.

Work 25 rows of St st on these 31 sts, slipping first st of every row.

Turn heel:

Row 1 K19, skpo, turn.

Row 2 P8, p2tog, turn.

Row 3 K9, skpo, turn.

Row 4 P10, p2tog, turn.

Cont in this way until all heel sts are on one needle. *19 sts.*

Working in the round again, k these 19 sts, then pick up and k 15 sts along side of heel flap; k across all 29 sts of instep onto one needle; pick up and k 15 sts down other side of heel flap; k across 10 sts from first needle; the next st is the beginning of a round. *78 sts.*

K sts on first and third needles and patt on second needle for instep as follows:

INSTEP

Round 1 (K3, sk2p, k3, yo, k1, yo) twice, k3, sk2p, k3.

Round 2 and every foll even-numbered round Knit.

Round 3 (K2, sk2p, k2, yo, k3, yo) twice, k2, sk2p, k2.

Round 5 (K1, sk2p, k1, yo, k5, yo) twice, k1, sk2p, k1.

Round 7 (Sk2p, yo, k7, yo) twice, sk2p.

Round 9 K1 (yo, k3, sk2p, k3, yo, k1) twice.

Round 11 First needle: k to last 3 sts, k2tog, k1; second needle: (k2, yo, k2, sk2p, k2, yo, k1) twice, k1; third needle: k1, ssk, k to end.

Round 13 Dec at end of first and beg of third needle as before; second needle: (k3, yo, k1, sk2p, k1, yo, k2) twice, k1.

Round 15 Dec as before; second needle: (k4, yo, sk2p, yo, k3) twice, k1.

Round 16 Knit. Cont to dec on alt rounds as before to 58 sts.

Round 17 Second needle: k2tog, k3, yo, k1, yo, k3, sk2p, k3, yo, k1, yo, k3, ssk.

Round 19 Second needle: k2tog, k2, yo, k3, yo, k2, sk2p, k2, yo, k3, yo, k2, ssk.

Round 21 Second needle: k2tog, k1, yo, k5, yo, k1, sk2p, k1, yo, k5, yo, k1, ssk.

Round 23 Second needle: k2tog, yo, k7, sk2p, yo, k7, yo, ssk.

Round 24 Knit.

Rep the patt on second needle from round 9 through round 24 once more, then cont in St st until foot measures 6½ [7, 7½] inches/16.5 [18, 19]cm from back of heel. Rearrange the sts so that there are 29 sts on second needle by taking 4 sts from each of the other two needles.

SHAPE TOE

Round 1 First needle: k to last 3 sts, k2tog, k1; second needle: k1, ssk, k to last 3 sts, k2tog, k1; third needle: k1, ssk, k to end.

Round 2 Knit.

Rep these 2 rounds to 26 sts; graft toe sts tog (see page 142) or bind off tog on the WS.

Make another sock in the same way.

FINISHING

Block or press carefully (see page 143).

Techniques

GAUGE

At the beginning of every pattern is a gauge measurement, such as "28 sts and 28 rows measure 4 inches/10cm over stockinette stitch using size 5/3.75mm needles." Only by matching this gauge can you produce a sock of the correct size. Several factors affect the gauge: needle size, stitch pattern, yarn, and the knitter.

Needle size Larger needles produce larger stitches, resulting in fewer stitches in the gauge swatch; smaller needles produce smaller stitches, so there will be more stitches in your gauge swatch. Note: The socks were knitted using metric needles; if you have trouble achieving the correct gauge, try using metric needles.

Stitch pattern Different stitch patterns produce different gauges, so you must check your gauge each time you embark on a new pattern, using the stitch pattern specified. If no pattern is specified, measure the gauge over stockinette stitch.

Yarn Patterns worked in finer yarns have more stitches and rows over a given measurement than those in thicker yarns. It is very important to check your gauge if you use a different yarn from that specified in the pattern, because even a standard weight of yarn can vary from one manufacturer to another. Even within the same brand of yarn, dark colors may produce fewer stitches over the given measurement than the lighter colors.

The knitter Even when using the same yarn, needle size, and stitch pattern, two knitters may not produce knitting at the same gauge because they knit with a different tension. If your gauge does not match that given in the pattern, you should change to a larger or smaller needle size.

Making a gauge swatch

1 Using the yarn, needles, and stitch pattern called for, knit a sample slightly larger than 4 inches/10cm square. Block the sample as the finished socks would be blocked (see page 143).

2 Being careful not to stretch it, lay the sample right side up on a flat surface and place a rigid ruler along one row. Use pins to mark the beginning and end of a 4-inch/10cm measurement. Count the number of stitches between the pins.

3 Place the ruler vertically along one side of a column of stitches, and mark your 4-inch/10cm measurement as before. Count the number of rows between the pins.

If you have fewer stitches and rows than given in the pattern, then you should use smaller needles; if there are more stitches and rows, you should try larger needles. As a rough guide, changing the needles

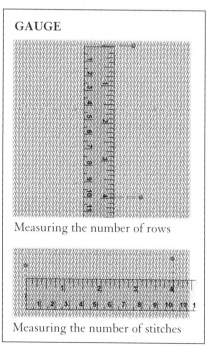

GAUGE

Measuring the number of rows

Measuring the number of stitches

CASTING ON

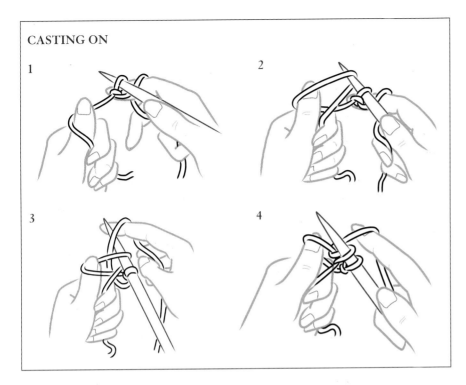

1

2

3

4

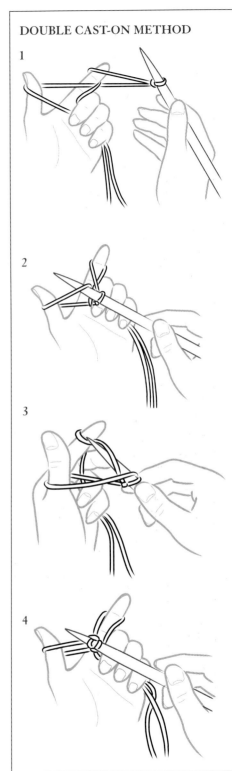

1

2

3

4

by one size makes a difference of about one stitch in every 2 inches/5cm.

If you cannot match both the stitch and row gauge, work to the correct stitch gauge, as the length can be adjusted by working more or fewer rows.

SPECIAL TECHNIQUES

Casting on

Casting on for top-down socks is best done using the thumb, or long-tail, cast-on method; this uses only one needle but produces the really elastic edge that is needed for socks. Leaving a "long tail" of yarn (about 1 inch/2.5cm for every stitch you want to make), make your slip knot on the needle as usual.

1 Hold your needle and working yarn in your right hand, and the tail end in your left hand, across the palm and looped over your thumb from back to front. The left thumb keeps the yarn at a slight tension.

2 Insert your needle under the tail of yarn that runs around your thumb.

3 Wrap the main yarn around the needle from back to front and draw it through the loop around your thumb.

4 Pull on the tail end of yarn to tighten the stitch on the needle. Repeat until you have cast on the number of stitches required. (Reverse the positions of yarn and needles if you are left-handed.)

Double cast-on method

If you knit with the yarn held in the left hand, you may prefer to use the double cast-on method (see right). This produces exactly the same flexible edge as the thumb method. Only one needle is used.

1 Wind the short end of yarn around your left thumb and the ball end around your fingers as shown in the drawing.

2 Slip the needle up through the loop on your thumb, then over the yarn going

around your index finger, rotating your left wrist toward you as you do so (this comes naturally), forming a loop (the new stitch) on the needle.

3 Let the thumb loop slide off the thumb, and tighten the stitch on the needle by pulling on the short end of yarn with your thumb.

Knitting in the round

Most of the socks in this book are knitted in the round. In this method, the front of the work always faces you, so it is easier to follow pattern charts, whether they are color- or stitch-pattern charts.

If you are using circular needles, cast on in the usual way and knit into the first stitch to make a continuous round. You must make certain that your cast-on row is not twisted when beginning your first round. To knit stockinette stitch, simply knit every row.

If you are using a set of four (or five) double-pointed needles, the stitches are divided among three (or four) of the needles, and the spare is used to knit. To close the circle, knit into the first cast-on

stitch and mark this stitch with a plastic marker or contrasting thread. As you knit, make sure no gap forms when you move from one needle to the next. If you find it difficult to avoid leaving gaps, you can rotate this point around the work by moving two or three stitches each time you change from one needle to another. If you do this, it is important to mark the center back of your work.

Stitch-pattern charts

Simple patterns containing only knit and purl, such as those used on the gansey stitch patterns (see pages 58–73), can be shown on charts. In our charts, a cross represents a purl stitch and a plain square a knit stitch. When knitting in the round, you have the right side facing, and you read every row of the chart from right to left.

Cables

A distinctive characteristic of several of our patterns is the use of cables. These are created when stitches are moved out of position, so that braided or ropelike twists are formed. This is achieved by using a special, double-pointed cable needle.

A given number of stitches are slipped onto the cable needle and held at either the front or the back of the work. A number of stitches are then worked from the main needle, then the stitches on the cable needle are worked.

Stitches held at the front twist a cable from right to left when knitted off; stitches held at the back twist the cable from left to right when knitted off.

Fair Isle and Argyle knitting

In order to knit Fair Isle and Argyle patterns, you need to follow a color-pattern chart and use two colors of yarn in a row.

Color-pattern charts

Color patterns are often given in the form of a chart, where each square represents one stitch, and each line of the chart represents one row or round. In this book the colors are indicated by colors corresponding to those used for the socks.

The chart is worked from bottom to top, and the rows are numbered with odd numbers on the right-hand side of the chart and even numbers on the left.

STITCH-PATTERN CHART

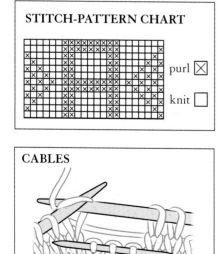

purl ☒

knit ☐

CABLES

A TYPICAL COLOR-PATTERN CHART

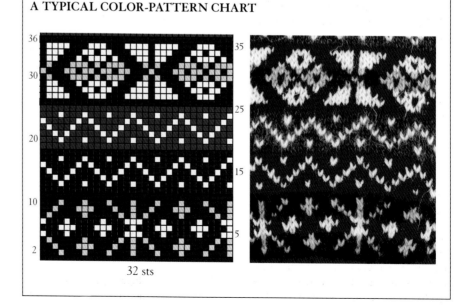

32 sts

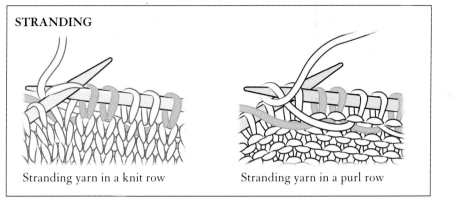

STRANDING

Stranding yarn in a knit row

Stranding yarn in a purl row

The same kind of chart is used for both circular and flat knitting, although it must be read differently.

In circular knitting, such as Fair Isle, every row on the chart represents a round of knitting; since you have the right side of the work facing you, every stitch will be a knit stitch and you read every row from right to left. Mark the beginning of each round with a stitch marker.

For flat knitting, such as Argyle or intarsia knitting, you will knit backward and forward in stockingette stitch, so the first row (and odd-numbered rows) will be knit and the chart read from right to left. These are right-side rows. The second row (and every even-numbered row) is worked in purl and the chart read from left to right; these are wrong-side rows.

Using two colors of yarn in a row

When knitting Fair Isle, the yarn that is not being used has to be carried across the back of the knitting. This is normally done by stranding; in Fair Isle there are not usually more than five stitches before a color change, so there are no long strands at the back of the fabric. The advantage of stranding is that the finished fabric is softer than when yarns are woven in; it is very important that the strands at the back of the work not be pulled too tightly, both to achieve the correct gauge (stranding too tightly will pucker the fabric) and so that

there is natural give in the finished knitting. To ensure this, every time you change color, gently but firmly pull back the last ten or so stitches on the right-hand needle to stretch your knitting very slightly.

In Fair Isle, always join the new color at the beginning of a round. Break off the old yarn leaving a few inches of spare yarn; join the new color and the finished color with a single knot, making sure the knot is close to the last stitch on your right-hand needle. Begin the next round; at the finishing stage turn the sock inside out and, using a large tapestry needle, weave the spare yarn into the first ten stitches of the round, then carefully trim away the excess.

In Argyle knitting, use a different ball for each diamond; twist the yarns around each other at the back of the work to avoid making a hole when changing colors.

Wrap and turn (short-row shaping)

With the knit side facing, work the number of stitches required. Slip the next stitch purlwise, bring the yarn to the front, and slip the stitch back onto the left needle. Turn, bring the yarn to the front, and work back along the row the required number of stitches.

With the purl side facing, slip the next stitch purlwise, take the yarn to the back,

and slip the stitch back onto the left needle. Turn, take the yarn to the back, and work the required number of stitches.

To work back over the stitches

To knit a wrapped stitch, insert the needle from the front to the back into the wrap, then knitwise into the stitch itself. Knit the wrap and the stitch together.

To purl a wrapped stitch, insert the needle into the back of the wrap, then purlwise into the stitch, and purl them together.

Closing the toe

The best way to close the toe of a top-down sock is either by using a three-needle bind-off or by grafting the stitches together, also called Kitchener stitch.

Three-needle bind-off

For the three-needle bind-off, first place the knitted pieces together; if you want the bind-off to be hidden, turn the socks inside out; if you want the bind-off to be a visible feature, place the pieces together with the wrong sides facing. Use the spare

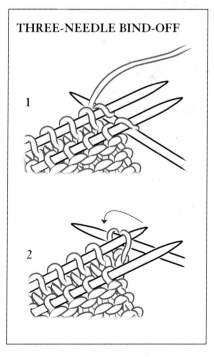

THREE-NEEDLE BIND-OFF

1

2

needle (third needle) to knit the first stitch off both the needles at the same time; repeat with the second stitches. When you have two stitches on your right-hand needle, take the first stitch over the second, as for binding off in the usual way. Repeat along the row until all stitches have been bound off.

Grafting, or Kitchener stitch

An even neater way of closing the toe is grafting, or Kitchener stitch, which makes an invisible seam. Thread some of your yarn into a tapestry (blunt-pointed) needle. Hold the two pieces of knitting together, still on their needles, with wrong sides together and needles pointing to the right. There must be an equal number of stitches on both needles.

To start, insert the tapestry needle into the first stitch on the front needle, as if

to purl, and pull the yarn through. With the tapestry needle, go through the first stitch on the back needle, as if to knit, and pull the yarn through. Keep the joining yarn at the same tension as the knitting.

1 Insert the tapestry needle in the first stitch on the front needle as if to knit, then slip the stitch off the knitting needle.

2 Sew into the next stitch on the front needle purlwise, pulling the yarn through at the same tension as the knitting.

3 On the back needle, sew through the first stitch purlwise and slip that from the needle. Note: A stitch gets dropped off the needle once you have passed the tapestry needle through it twice.

4 Sew knitwise into the next stitch on the back needle, and repeat steps 1–4

until you have only one stitch remaining on each needle.

Now work step 2 and step 3 again, reading "first stitch" as "remaining stitch."

Toe-up socks

Socks that are cast on at the toe and knitted upward are found in various places around the world, and our Egyptian and Turkish patterns (see pages 38 and 46), both use this method.

To cast on, you need a set of four double-pointed needles.

1 Hold two of your needles together with the points even and with the yarn at the front; wrap the yarn around each needle to form a figure-eight between the two needles until you have the desired number of stitches on each needle. Hold the end of the yarn down with your left thumb.

2 Using a third needle, knit all the stitches along the top needle; try not to let the loops on the lower needle become too loose; but if they do, they can be tightened later with the tip of a needle.

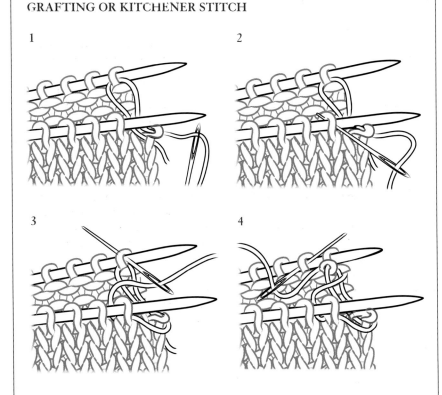

GRAFTING OR KITCHENER STITCH

1

2

3

4

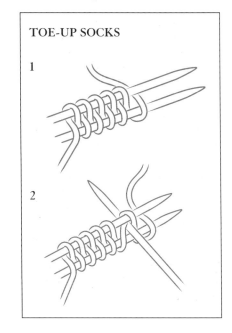

TOE-UP SOCKS

1

2

3 Turn your work and, using the spare needle, knit all the loops off the bottom needle; you will have to knit into the backs of these loops to prevent them from being twisted.

Knit each needle one more time; there will be four rows of knitting between your two needles.

Your cast-on is complete. Work any increase row as instructed and then continue with your chosen pattern, knitting in the round.

FINISHING

Blocking

When you have finished knitting, your socks have to be blocked. If they have been knitted in the round, they can be blocked as they are. Argyle and intarsia socks have to be sewn together first.

The blocking surface can be the ironing board, covered with a piece of cotton fabric or terry cloth, but it is a good idea to use purchased sock blockers, which are available in different sizes. Pull the socks over the blockers, then spray them with cold, clean water, using a spray bottle, until they are just damp- not soaked-and leave them to dry naturally on the blockers.

Blockers are particularly useful if your socks are knitted without shaping in the leg, like the Fair Isle socks on pages 76 and 80; blockers help to make the ankle narrower and the leg wider. Shetland knitters always wash their sock as part of the finishing process and dry them on their own shaped blockers, which they call "sock boards."

Lacy wool socks also benefit from the use of sock blockers, which help to maintain the openwork effect.

Blocking is also an excellent method of restoring your socks to their original shape after washing. Roll the socks in a towel to remove excess moisture, put the damp socks on the blockers, and leave them to dry naturally.

If you don't have sock blockers, ease the damp socks into the correct shape with your hands, flattening them slightly, and allow them to dry naturally. The Turkish socks with peasant heel (see page 46) cannot be dried on blockers, but straight pieces of firm cardboard, cut to the correct size, could be used in the leg and foot, with the side bands placed at the edges of the cardboard.

An alternative method is to lay the socks on your blocking surface and ease them into the correct shape with your hands. Then hold a hot steam iron over the surface, so that it is barely touching the knitting, and allow the steam to penetrate. Let the socks dry naturally.

Seams

If your socks require a seam, the most versatile stitch for sewing up is a version of mattress stitch; this provides a strong, invisible seam (see above right).

Place the two seam edges side by side with right sides facing you. With a tapestry needle and matching yarn, stitch through one stitch bar only, half a stitch in from the edge. Pick up one stitch bar, as close to the edge as possible, on the other side. Without pulling the stitches taut, pick up the next stitch bar on the first side. Then pick up the next stitch bar on the other side, and so on.

When the thread is looped from one edge to the other a few times, pull it taut gently and the edges will be pulled together. Continue until the seam is complete.

SEAMS

Washing

After spending a lot of time and trouble hand-knitting socks, it pays to wash them with care. Always check the yarn label for washing instructions, and keep one label for reference. A lot of yarns now can be safely machine washed (these are often marked "super wash." The main exception is Shetland yarn, which must be hand-washed.

Using a wool detergent and hand-warm water, gently immerse the socks and squeeze them in the suds for a few minutes. Do not rub or soak. Rinse in the same temperature of water several times to remove all the detergent and until the rinse water is absolutely clear.

Place the socks in a thick towel and roll it up. Press the roll with your hands to remove as much water as possible. Then spread the damp socks on a clean towel on a rack over the bathtub or on a freestanding drying rack and allow them to dry naturally.

Sock blockers can be used to keep your socks the perfect size after washing (see above).

Resources

Easyknits.co.uk
www.easyknits.co.uk
info@easyknits.co.uk
For a pack of Bamboo-Merino mix
dyed for the Traditional Shetland
Pattern Socks on page 97

Iriss of Penzance
66 Chapel Street, Penzance,
Cornwall, TR18 4AD
UK
+ 44 (0)1736 366 568
www.iriss.co.uk/ganseys
sales@iriss.co.uk
For Wendy (Poppleton's)
5-ply Guernsey wool
For British Breeds 5-ply
Guernsey wool

Jamieson & Smith (Shetland Wool Brokers) Ltd
90 North Road, Lerwick,
Shetland Isles, ZE1 0PQ
UK
+ 44 (0)1595 693 579
www.shetland-wool-
brokers.zetnet.co.uk
sales@shetlandwoolbrokers.co.uk

Jamieson's of Shetland
Sandness Industrial Estate,
Sandness, Shetland Isles,
ZE2 9PL
UK
+ 44 (0)1595 693 114
www.jamiesonsshetland.co.uk
info@jamiesonsofshetland.co.uk

Schoolhouse Press
6899 Cary Bluff,
Pittsville, WI 54466
USA
+ 1 800.850.5648
www.schoolhousepress.com
info@schoolhousepress.com
For Jamieson & Smith Shetland
yarns, and Poppleton's
Guernsey wool

Simply Shetland
18375 Olympic Avenue South,
Seattle, WA 98188
USA
+ 1 887.743.8526
www.simplyshetland.net
info@simplyshetland.net
For Jamieson's Shetland Spindrift

The Yarn Barn
5077 Andersonville Road,
Dillwyn, VA 23936
USA
+ 1 800.850.6008
www.yarnbarn.com
info@yarnbarn.com
For Debbie Bliss and Rowan Yarns
For Jamieson's Shetland Spindrift
For Jamieson & Smith
Shetland yarns

Westminster Fibers Inc.
165 Ledge Street,
Nashua, NH 03060
USA
+ 1 800.445.9272
www.westminsterfibers.com
For your nearest stockist of
Rowan yarns

Acknowledgments

A big thank you to Jacqui Small and her team, especially Zia Mattocks and Kerenza Swift, and to Barbara Zuñiga and Simon Brown for making the book so beautiful.

Boundless thanks go to the knitters, especially Rita Taylor, who wrote patterns, knitted as well as rescued other knitters, and who advised on the Techniques section; to Susan Smith who checked patterns; and to Paula Hornsby who trawled her collection of vintage patterns for me, and gave the benefit of her advice. This book would also have been the poorer but for Margaret Stuart, who found a knitter on Shetland able to knit the lovely Fair Isle socks on pages 76 and 80, re-creating these old patterns.

KNITTERS
Cables
Debbie Abrahams
Jean Molloy
Rita Taylor
Joyce Coombs

Stripes & Multicolor
Sasha Kagan
Susan Smith
Helen Llamas
Pauline Hornsby
Lou Sugg

Gansey Stitch Patterns
Hilary Grundy
Margaret MacInnes
Rita Taylor

Fair Isle & Sanquhar
Mhairi Sinclair
Julia Smith
Jan Ter Heide

Argyle
Paulette Burgess
Rita Taylor
Charlotte Lodge

Lace Knitting
Helen Scott
Sarah Crowther
Rita Taylor

The publishers would like to thank Toast for the kind loan of clothes for the photo-shoot (see website for current collection and store information www.toast.co.uk; order on +44 (0)844 557 5200; contact@toast.co.uk). Thanks also to Rosemary Barlow for the loan of vintage gardening tools and props.